Facing Life  Na

Penumbra Press · Manotick, ON

PENUMBRA PRESS
Box 940 · Manotick, ON
Canada · K4M 1A8

Printed & bound in Canada

Penumbra Press gratefully acknowledges
the financial support of the Government
of Canada through the Book Publishing
Industry Development Program (BPIDP)
for our publishing activities. We also
acknowledge the Government of Ontario
through the Ontario Media Development
Corporation's Ontario Book Initiative.

LIBRARY AND ARCHIVES CANADA
CATALOGUING IN PUBLICATION

Brown, Nancy, 1945–
     Facing life / Nancy Brown.

ISBN 978-1-897323-08-3

1. Brown, Nancy, 1945–
2. Addicts—Rehabilitation
3. Substance abuse
4. Twelve-step programs.
5. Addicts—Biography
I. Title

RC564.B764 2007
616.86'03   C2007-902408-4

For all those two-legged and four-legged angels,
earthbound and otherwise, who carried me until the miracle.

And to myself: lost and found.

Contents

Acknowledgements

I would like to express my heartfelt thanks to John Flood, my publisher, for making it possible for the message contained in the tragedies and joys of my life to reach those who still suffer from the disease of addiction.

I would like to thank Dr. Raju Hajela for so many things that it would make its own book. And for the title of this book. My deep and enduring gratitude to you, dear Lamplighter.

Thanks to my family, Peter and Ann, David and Linda, Susan and Francisco, for their support, and for never once censoring my words. To the Tuesday night writers' group for taking me under its wing, and for a four-year creative writing lesson. To the Monday afternoon therapy group for its brutal honesty and grit in the difficult times. I could not have done it without you. To my dear and steadfast friends, whose open ears and patient hearts eased my frantic mind and soothed my injured spirit. And to all those who read those excruciating first drafts. To my many editors for their unique and valuable contributions to the development and polishing of this work and for the opportunities for personal growth nestled therein: Dr. Hajela, my first editor, who helped me weed out the addict-thinking in the first drafts; Brian Henry, who helped me believe that my personal story had merit; Maureen Garvie, dear friend—I see your face on every page; and Douglas Campbell, whose laser insight and generous heart nudged me to go deeper and made it fun. To Martin Kauffman and Pierre Landry for rescuing me from the computer crazies.

Piano

Fine wooden planks
Pale ivory's gleam
A heart that sings
While fingers weep.
The cradle deep
Within your bones
Rocks the weary past to sleep.

NANCY BROWN

Foreword

Beginning as far back as I can remember, I was absolutely certain that I was insane. But I wasn't. I was suffering from a disease called addiction. My experience of sexual abuse, which had begun at the age of five, gave rise to a profound sense of shame and a conviction that I was bad, dirty, worthless. I soon discovered that I could suppress these feelings for a time by swallowing various substances. This pattern of behaviour was locked in and reinforced by a genetic predisposition to addiction.

My life became my tragedy, but I didn't know how to take responsibility for it. For decades, so-called experts told me that my problems were directly related to my sexual abuse, and I believed them. Admittedly, the abuse was responsible for having left me fear-based and shame-based, but what I didn't understand was that it was not the direct or exclusive cause of my difficulties as an adult.

As time passed, I found more powerful substances to swallow to muffle the din of childhood secrets, unexpressed feelings, and the devastation that my addictive acting-out brought to my life. I continued to swallow until I was convinced that I was undeserving of anything good or beautiful. On my fiftieth birthday, I counted the pills I'd been saving and decided that I had enough.

§

I took my last drink in February of 1998. It was then that the idea of a book began to percolate. It would be my story, a portrait of addiction—hope-dasher, dream-smasher, merciless shredder of self-respect. Perhaps by becoming a published author I would show those I loved that I was something other than a glaring familial anomaly, a shameful burden, a failure trailing a lifetime of tragedy.

In the following months, as my recovery process began to take hold, many things became clear. Addiction is an incurable disease. Instead of continually fighting a battle I could not win,

I would have to lay down my armour and admit to my powerlessness over drugs and alcohol. I would have to come to know my adversary so well that I could accept it as a partner in my struggle to achieve wellness.

On January 1, 2001, I began to write my memoir. My motive now was more in line with my recovery goals. Although I still longed to be a somebody in the eyes of the world, I now understood that first of all I had to tell my story to and for myself—tell it as it happened, not as addiction would distort it. And heal by the telling.

§

There is overwhelming evidence that addiction impinges upon most lives in some way. In spite of this, few written accounts have adopted a personal perspective, particularly a woman's. One reason for this gaping hole on bookstore shelves is shame, and the stigma that still surrounds this greatly misunderstood disease. My book has been written to help redress the silence.

I am an addict who nearly destroyed herself because she didn't know how not to. The Alcoholics Anonymous fellowship and a rigorous commitment to its Twelve-Step philosophy gave me the tools I needed to face my life head-on. Healing is possible for all who have travelled my path, but it cannot endure without the truth. For me that has meant accepting my past and my own flawed humanity—all of it.

I have found my wings at last. Come fly with me.

1 · The Big Yellow Truck

My mother said my lips looked like a rosebud when she first saw me in the hospital. She brought me home to the house where I grew up wrapped in a pink blanket embroidered with tiny yellow flowers. Ten years ago, bereft of hope and as desperate as I had ever been, I felt compelled to make a trip to the basement to find that blanket and bring it up to bed with me, a journey that seemed a thousand miles.

When I was small, our house was an adventure, a mysterious journey unfolding endlessly in wonderful surprises. I didn't believe Dad when he said the fireplace chimney went right up to the sky. But one day a starling fell through, squawking, flapping, making an awful mess, so I knew it was true, because birds always come from the sky. That day I knew for sure that my father would never lie to me. I believed him then, and I believed him forty years later when he told me to my face that he didn't love me anymore.

On the top floor of our house there were so many rooms I sometimes forgot where they all were. Mom rented some of them to overflow guests from the hotels, but I hated her having to launder sheets every day in a creaky wringer washer in the back shed and wash and wax the wood floors. Once I hid the scrub brush with splayed bristles that looked like a giant's worn-out toothbrush so she wouldn't have to.

I liked the back shed best of all. It had lots of shelves and drawers that I wasn't supposed to open but did every chance I got. There were strange rusty things inside that made me want to make up stories about them. Some wound up or laced up. Some cranked up or zipped up. Some things whirred and buzzed, rattled and crackled, and one mysterious round thing Dad said was a dried-out gourd sounded as if it had sand sifting inside. Once I found a doorknob and pretended it belonged on a door to a secret room where bad things never happened.

My father was a mountain, tall and stout, with long, strong arms that bent like a hammock. He'd lift me up and place me

on his giant foot, and I'd climb him, stopping on my way to
play horsy on his knee or rest on his belly. My favourite place
was scooped out, soft and smooth, and it smelled like Three
Roses shaving cream. When I buried my face there, I heard my
very own father heart thump-thump in the side of his neck. It
was a place sweet and pure, where forever-love is born.

My mother was smooth and straight-up tall. Her face was
square and open like a picture book I never got tired of looking at. It reminded me of a face I saw on an old coin once,
plain and proud, not all dolled-up fussy like some mothers'.
Her lap was a cradle of warmth after I fell down and thought
I'd never be able to stop crying. Her quick hands put the Band-
Aid on my knee, while her mouth made soft cooing sounds.
She also cooked the best chicken and dumplings in the world.
She was smart, too, for when she read me stories and I asked
a million questions, her answers were long and thoughtful,
and filled me with wonder.

Mom was always doing something to make me feel important. She knit my black and yellow bumblebee mittens that
were attached by a long string, and when I wasn't wearing
them she would hang them carefully on nails hammered into
the wall at the bottom of the back stairs. She sewed countless
buttons, darned our socks and sweaters, and stood at the sink
late at night preparing junket for me when I was sick.

When I was four, my parents noticed that my left foot
dragged a little and flipped inward at each step. Dr. Bingham,
who was even taller than Dad and talked like Winston
Churchill, said I'd had a mild case of polio. He said I should
walk as little as possible for six months to give my leg a rest. My
mother pushed me everywhere in a baby carriage, even though
I wasn't a baby at all. Though she rarely said the words, I knew
she loved me, even in the end, when I wasn't very lovable at all.

My brother was the cutest boy on the block, with an angel-
scamp smile that made my heart do somersaults. That hasn't
changed much. Peter was fascinated by bugs, and could often
be found bent over, peering into the grass, a pint-sized ento-
mologist looking for something icky to put in a jar.

I was more interested in stray kittens. When I brought them home, I hid them in boxes with holes poked through the sides for air, so Mom wouldn't find them. But she always did. Sometimes she let me keep them and sometimes she didn't.

Dad came into the kitchen one day with a big grin on his face and pulled out of his policeman's coat pocket a squirmy tangle of wavy-red fur. We named him Rusty. He had long fluffy hair under his tail that Mom called pantaloons, and when he was happy he wiggled his back end so hard he fell down.

I loved Rusty almost as much as my family, and told him everything. Once, later on, I whispered into his ear that I was mad at God for not keeping his promises. Mom told me God looked after all little children, but I thought he must be busy, for he seemed to have forgotten about me. I knew Rusty was listening, because he sat very still, cocked his head to one side, and looked right into my eyes.

§

When I was five, a dusty black car stopped in front of the house across the street. From my perch at the front window, I saw two grown-ups and two children get out. Soon after, a big yellow truck parked behind the car.

The man had a big belly and not much hair. Beside him stood a small, pretty woman. But her shoulders were hunched —nothing like my mother's, which were square and even, like the top of our new refrigerator. A young boy hopped out who reminded me of the grasshoppers Peter caught last summer, all knees and elbows, with ears so big they looked like wings attached to the side of his head.

Then I saw her, the most beautiful little girl I'd ever seen. She had long, crow-black curls, fawn eyes, and skin the colour of creamed coffee. But even from across the street, I noticed that her mouth turned down in the corners.

"Hallayoollya!" I whooped through the window. "Hallayoooooooollya!" I hollered again—that queer word from church that made my tongue bounce around in my mouth and meant that a wonderful thing had just happened. "I'll let her play with my new kitten Tink if she lets me be her friend," I said to Rusty. He wagged his tail and made a funny squeak that wasn't quite a bark yet because he was still a puppy. "Maybe that will make her smile."

A few days later, Mom, Dad, and I walked across the street to our new neighbours' house. Mom carried a freshly baked ginger cake and let me hold the caramel sauce that went on top. It was in a pickle jar that had been rinsed out.

We sat in the front room and talked about the television, the first one I'd seen up close. The plain black box with the glass front and knobs along the side sat in the corner with a vase of plastic flowers on top. All the kids at school wanted their parents to get one, but it didn't look like anything special to me. The man smiled as if he'd forgotten what he was doing halfway through, and said I could come over any time to watch it. But I didn't care about that. I couldn't keep my eyes off Ruthie.

She was quiet and limp-still, as if she was sleeping with her eyes open. Seeing her droopy like that made me want to cheer her up. Maybe I could show her Dad's cushion that made a rude noise when he sat on it.

The woman had black circles under her eyes and didn't look happy we were there. The lemonade we drank from plastic glasses was so sour it made my tongue curl. The cookies came from a store and tasted mouldy. Why couldn't we have a piece of the ginger cake instead?

We said goodbye and walked home across the street with Mom and Dad each holding one of my hands. My father made my fist into a ball and wrapped his whole hand around mine.

"They seemed like respectable folks," he said. "Hard-working, too."

"The children seemed well-behaved," replied Mom. They lifted me up onto the curb, swinging me a little just for fun.

"Not like some little girls I know." Dad winked down his nose at me to show he was joking. "A good idea of his to rent those six rooms on the top floors. Says he'll rent them to single chaps from the Aluminum Plant. Shows he's a head for business. It'll take a lot to get those rooms in shape by fall."

I couldn't stop thinking about Ruthie's eyes. That night I dreamed her face was a dead fish's, like the ones Dad brought home in a pail. The swollen, staring-dead eyes were hers. When I told Mom, she said, "Don't worry your pretty little head about it. It's hard for children to move and leave their friends behind."

Mom and Dad visited back and forth all summer with the new neighbours. They must have seemed nice, because I heard Mom say it was good to know there was a respectable family nearby to babysit me. My parents were building a cottage and couldn't always take me with them. Peter already had a French sitter, Marie, and I loved the way she made her words sound like music. I wished I could go with him, but Mom said two children would be a handful.

One night she took me by the hand to the house across the street to spend my first night with the new family. The lady with the round shoulders met me at the door, but didn't look happy to see me.

"Be a good girl, honey," Mom said. She kissed me goodbye, then she ran her finger down my nose and tickled me under my chin. "I'll pick you up first thing in the morning."

I walked through the pretty stained-glass door and dropped off the edge of my world.

2 · The Bad Place

The house across the street was a big fat liar. It pretended to be a nice old brick house with a stained-glass door that sparkled in the sun. But it wasn't. It was a smoky forest of tree-trunk men with petrified hearts, sharp fingernails on grasping fingers, and smelly flannel shirt-tails that dangled around my head.

In that house a biting tangle of fear and helplessness grew in my throat and stuck there as if it owned me. It made a dreadful sound, and I searched my whole life for something to swallow that would make it stop.

One day I came back home from that house sore all over. Mom had put a fresh batch of maple walnut fudge on the rose candy plate with the smooth, scalloped edges. When I grabbed two pieces, she gave me a look that meant I should only take one. I made a beeline up the steep-narrow back stairs anyway and crawled into Mom's closet so she wouldn't hear me cry. I wouldn't let the bad man hear me cry, either, even when he said Peter and Rusty would wish they'd never been born if I didn't shut up and stop wiggling. Once I made a noise when it hurt, and he said he'd skin Rusty alive if I didn't stop. Crouched in the dark, cold and shivery, I stuffed the candy into my mouth, chewing frantically, juice running down my chin.

Soon I started stealing candy from little corner stores in my neighbourhood. They were glorious gardens, with rows and rows of jars and bins of every-colour-of-the-rainbow candy, where I could pick and pluck to my heart's content. I'd stuff my pockets and run home to hide it in the back of the closet.

I spent a lot of time there. The clothes brushing against my face reminded me of the bad man's shirt-tails, so I pretended the closet was a jungle and the clothes were tree boughs. I imagined monkeys swinging from tree to tree snatching pieces of candy from my hand. I didn't mind. They were my friends, and always came to the closet when I was afraid. They seemed to like the soft chewy banana treats the best.

There in the almost-dark I made a connection that would last a lifetime. As the sweetness slid down my throat and sleep tugged at my eyelids, I found that I wasn't afraid any more.

§

I have three happy memories from childhood. I'm sure there are more, but the bad ones have smudged them over.

The first is climbing my father-mountain, where I nuzzled my face into his neck and felt so safe.

The second is the trip our family made several times a year out Perth Road to Bedford Mills, where Dad was born and my aunts lived. All the turns and hills on the road made my stomach do something Mom called "boiling over." This made the car stink, but no one was ever mad at me, even when they had to stop the car and scrub up the mess.

While Mom and Peter walked up the hill to see Aunt Cecile, Dad led me over to the stone mill on the edge of Bedford Pond. I loved the feeling of being special, the feeling that it was only the two of us who could play that game we played by the water's edge. He'd throw his arm out in an arc that included everything, as far as the eye could see. "Nancy," he'd say, "if you and I were in a boat, we could sail right out to the ocean from this spot."

When the wind rippled the water, the white water lilies bobbed and swayed. They disappeared for a second or two, then popped up again like white ducks. Sometimes there were real ducks, and Dad always brought a bag of crumbs to feed to them. He would let me hold the bag, and sometimes I would try to throw the bread to the ducks. I threw it as far as I could but it never reached them. Dad didn't mind though. When he tossed a crumb in the air and caught it in his mouth and then made quacking sounds, I squealed with delight.

Then, my very own mountain led me by his rough, dinner-plate hand away from the mill and up the twisting ribbon road to my aunt's house. I was happy then, a little girl in pigtails wearing my best red-plaid pleated skirt and my white tights with the baggy knees that wouldn't stay up no matter how I tugged at them.

The third happy memory was Christmas 1950, just before the big yellow truck came. The towering pine stood in the front room covered with tinsel, round, jiggling balls, and popcorn strings I'd made almost by myself. Rusty threw up that morning, a mess of gold, silver, red, and green, just like the colours on the tree. Mom bent over the branches, moving things up out of the way so he wouldn't eat any more.

The dollhouse I'd prayed for all year was next to the radiator, all tinny, brand-new, and painted in pink, with gold sparkles on the roof. Santa gave me a stuffed dog with a zipper in his stomach—a cloth-Rusty. Mom said I was supposed to put my pajamas in him, but I knew I wouldn't. It didn't seem right to stuff clothes into something that looked so real.

My Christmas stocking was filled with candy canes, a chocolate Santa, my favourite shortbread cookies with sprinkles, and an orange. I couldn't eat the orange after Dad told us his family was so poor that once all he got for Christmas was an orange, the only one he'd get to eat all year. When he said he ate the skin to make it last as long as he could, I felt sad.

We were sitting in the front room by the fire, and the crackling warmth made me feel safe. Peter was making an awful racket with his new dump truck. Mom was reading a new book she'd got. The pearls Dad had given her on their wedding day ("Delta pearls," Mom called them) framed her swanneck. Her hair had been bobby-pinned that morning, and I loved the way she made the waves hug her forehead. Dad rolled down onto the floor from his chair with a thump and a whoop, which meant that it was time to play our game. He scooped me up and wrapped my legs and arms around his neck. I was the elephant's trunk as he swayed and snorted, pounding the floor and making elephant sounds. We grunted and huffed, romped and stomped, laughing with such delight that Mom said, "Be careful, Dad, be careful."

He almost let me fall, but I forgave him. I forgave him everything back then: for pretending to be Santa Claus, for wearing that dark policeman's uniform, even for dropping a fish on my foot one day when he was cleaning bullheads for Saturday supper.

§

After the family moved in across the street, I began a ritual that our family talked about years later as if it was funny or cute. I'd drop my clothes in a pile on the front stoop and run around the block naked, head down, arms hammering the air in frantic circles. When I was an adult, Mom told me she used to get phone calls from around the neighbourhood. "Carmel, Nancy just turned west on Johnson Street, naked as a jay bird," or "Nancy just passed my verandah, heading for the coal yard without a stitch on. She'll cut her feet."

Who knows what I was trying to say by doing that? Maybe it was, "Please, please, look at me. Can't anyone see the red handprints?"

§

I was only five then, but something happened three years later that nobody thought was funny at all. Up till then we had spent the summers at our cottage, but this year I was supposed to go to girls' camp for the first time. I worried I wouldn't be able to steal enough candy for two weeks, let alone sneak it into the suitcase Mom would pack for me, but I had an idea. Cloth-Rusty's stomach would be the perfect spot to hide things, and the rest I could stuff in my bookbag. Mom never looked there when school was out. At the camp we stayed in cabins, several girls in each. I chose the top bunk so that I could eat my candy out of sight.

We had swimming and water-safety classes on tippy docks along the shoreline, like crocodiles all in a row. It was on one of those docks that I did something everyone thought was very, very bad. Swimming classes were over for the day and we had free time, so my friend Jane and I went down to the water to look for turtles. We weren't supposed to be there, but it was fun to have a secret. A counsellor discovered me taking Jane's bathing suit off. Jane didn't seem to mind. I didn't hurt her. I'd done it lots of times with Ruthie in the house across the street. The bad man showed me how.

The snooty counsellor grabbed my hand and dragged me to the office so fast my feet couldn't keep up. I couldn't understand what all the fuss was about. They called my parents and asked them to come and take me home.

In the back seat of my father's car I felt small. I wanted to puff up, but instead I shoved into the corner as far as I could. The car smelled oily, like my father's tool chest, and the windows were way up high like the ones at church. I flattened my palms together, pointed my fingers just right and prayed to God for Mom to start humming her favourite song, so I'd know she wasn't mad at me.

But my mother was silent. And for the first time I saw the look on my father's face in the rear-view mirror, the look that grew and grew over the years like a spreading stain. The sticky air clung like cobwebs, and I was sick in the place my heart was.

At the cottage the blinds were pulled, and I was kept inside until my camp time would have ended so that no one would know I'd been sent home. No one was invited to visit. No one was allowed to come inside. No one told me what I'd done that was so bad. I lay on my bed listening to the crunch of gravel as people passed on the road. As long as I live, I'll never forget my parents whispering. I was afraid they would send me away to a place for bad little girls.

When the blinds were finally opened, I crept outside, head hanging, a dirty rag of a thing. The first thing I did was head for the store in my bare feet to buy some penny candy, clutching the coin so tightly it left marks. I carried the candy down to the dock in a small brown-paper bag.

Leaning over the side of our green rowboat, I drew hearts in the water and watched the fish scramble at the bubbles. I wished I could chop myself in two and hide the part that made the bad man like me. When I was sure no one was looking, I crammed the candy into my mouth, chewing so hard and fast my mouth bled. The sooner I swallowed, the better I'd feel. Everything would be all right as long as I didn't stop.

§

And I didn't. The bad man didn't stop, either, until I made him, three years later, when I was eleven. I was tired of hurting *down there* all the time. I wanted to run away, but I couldn't leave Peter and Rusty with no one to protect them. And Mom and Dad would miss me, even though I worried them. Once, hidden at the top of the stairs, I heard them talking. They'd found the other candy-hiding places in the back shed, under the bed, and in the toes of my winter boots. They said my behaviour was strange, that I was always hungry and ate enough for two grown men.

It was all *his* fault. By now I knew enough not to go into the narrow hallway when I called on Ruthie. But this time he heard me and came to the door. When I was smaller, he often trapped me inside the two beautiful stained-glass doors that enclosed the vestibule. It doesn't seem right that such dreadful things happened between those two lovely panels. He wasn't wearing a shirt, and smelled the same as he always had, like our toilet before Mom cleaned it on Saturdays. That stink followed me everywhere, and sometimes I couldn't get it out of my nose, even after a whole bag of candy.

The bad man looked at me smugly, as if he hadn't sensed the difference in me. I wasn't small any more. Neither was Peter, and Rusty had been put to sleep. I wasn't going to take it any more and that was that. When he tried to put his hands on me I fought as hard as I could. A wild commotion of arms and legs, I hurled myself at him, trying to take my body back from that hulking, stinking coward. I bit a chunk of flesh from his arm, making him pay for all the years he had taken from me, hurting him as he'd hurt me. I remember the taste of his blood. I remember exactly what I said, slamming the words at him, wanting him to be afraid the same way I was: "I'm going to tell my father on you. He'll put you in jail. Peter will bash your brains in. You'd better watch out."

I still remember the look of fear on his face.

3 · The Hill

I didn't feel like a young girl. And my friends certainly didn't look the way I felt—old, and worn down by secret things. They seemed light and feathery, hardly touching the ground at all. My body felt pushed in, and bent-over heavy like my poor Aunt Ruby. When people looked at me I stared at my feet. I couldn't bear to look at their faces and know that they could see me as I was: a worn, animal thing, furtive, crouching, waiting for the next red handprint.

I was almost twelve, going into Grade Eight. On the first day of class the neighbourhood was buzzing with what-to-wear worries and who-would-the-teacher-be woes. My concerns were different.

I tried not to, but I had to take it everywhere: the memory of six-and-a-half years of loose flesh sprawled on me, the stain of madness, left to dry like tainted egg white. I remembered the dreaded ritual of smelly, hard things pressed into my mouth, choking me until I thought I'd die, and the raspy threats against Peter and Rusty that were slobbered into my ears. My head hung. My shoulders folded in. I was so tired.

I'd learned not to turn and look when I passed store windows, not to stare at my face in the mirror as I did my hair. But mirrors don't lie. I was fat and ugly. I wished I was dead. That summer, I'd watched the slender girls walking past my house wearing the latest styles and "look at me" smiles. I knew that none of the outfits in Purdy's Young Miss Shop would fit me. They were for the beautiful ones.

As I gazed long and hard into the angry glass, I remembered my mother's friend confiding with her over a cup of tea. "Carmel, it's a miracle," she said. "One pill and you're not hungry all day."

Maybe I wouldn't want to eat so much candy, and could be thin, like the other girls. I pleaded with my parents, and they agreed to let me try the pills. A doctor with crooked teeth and a droopy rag of a smile passed my mother a piece of white paper. The paper held a promise. The ugly duckling would vanish.

The miracle's name was Dexedrine.

§

I'd taken the first orange pill at breakfast. Now I was trudging the several blocks up the hill to Victoria School. Way up ahead I noticed the other kids dotting the street in their bright colours. I passed a group of younger girls playing hopscotch, jumping in the air and showing their frilly first-day slips. When they landed on the squares they tapped their toes on the numbers as if they owned the whole wide world. They pranced with their chins high, ribbons trailing from their glossy hair, and I knew by the way they moved that we were different, that they hadn't done the dreadful things I had.

But halfway up the hill I seemed to change, as though I had been dipped in a golden wash. My polio foot flip-flopped less. I could hardly feel the welts around my waist from my too-tight clothes. My shoulders straightened. My chin came up. I felt like a queen, and that title demanded a certain regal bearing.

I didn't want the candy tucked in my school bag. In fact I wasn't the least bit hungry, and couldn't remember why I'd felt so tired. It must be that pretty pill I took. The fear of not being good enough for my new school chums decreased with every step. I felt proud and strong, pretty and clean, and a little foolish for having fussed so much about the first day of school. My dirty secrets flew away in the clear fall air.

The next morning I felt guilty when I swallowed not one but two pills. But that quickly disappeared as the pill dissolved into my bloodstream. One thing I knew for sure: if I stopped taking them, I'd become ugly again. I was quickly learning the drug's power. A small orange demon was transforming my hell on earth into a dream come true.

The forgetting time of my life had begun.

4 · Aqua Vitae

The school year was almost over. I still felt like a big foot trying to squeeze into a too-tight world. Everything pinched: every friendship, every dream, every comment—even if it sounded nice. My clothes pinched, my father's look of disapproval pinched, but mostly my heart pinched. There was a crack in it that was widening, deepening. Sometimes it felt as if it would split in two and never stop bleeding—not the blood you can see, but the invisible kind that spilled over everything I saw and did.

The pills helped, but the golden veil that draped over everything when I took one didn't last very long, and sometimes my supply ran out before the prescription renewal date. I was worried I'd get fat again and look the way I felt on the inside. Then I discovered something else, something new to swallow when the pills were gone.

At a friend's birthday party I tried to join the huddled camaraderie, but didn't feel comfortable. And I was bored silly by all the giggling over Elvis Presley's latest record. Ruthie and Shirley were showing off the latest jitterbug moves, their full skirts whirling, their arms whipping as they swung each other around, breathless, red-cheeked, lost in a rock 'n' roll frenzy. Ruthie was so crazy about Elvis she told me she fainted once at the movies from screaming so much. I could never understand why Ruthie didn't look the way I felt. I know her father hurt her too. I had seen it with my own eyes. Maybe she forgot, so that she wouldn't die from remembering. I would never forget. I wouldn't give him the satisfaction.

My friend Michael was sitting in the corner. When I went over, he produced a silver flask from his pocket, took a swallow, and made a nasty-taste face. "Have a swig, Nance," he said, passing me the flask and puffing his chest out as if he'd handed me the world. Wanting him to like me, I reached for the flask.

It smelled like my parents' before-dinner drink, and reminded me that they seemed to like themselves better after they'd had one. Their faces lost their scrunched-up look and their laughs echoed off the walls. They stopped tugging at their clothes, crossing and uncrossing their legs, and pretending they weren't looking at you when they really were. When I swallowed, the liquid burned its way down like a hot, lazy snake, and soon the most wonderful thing happened. It felt as though my fairy godmother had finally noticed my needing her and, in one swift act of pity and kindness, flicked her wand. I forgot I was the fattest girl in the room. I forgot about the despicable things I'd done in the house across the street. And I forgot the bad-man smell that followed me everywhere. My world hardly pinched at all.

That night in bed I didn't worry about my "erratic" behaviour, as Dad put it, my acting so "out of character." I didn't lie awake feeling chopped into pieces: secret-keeper, pill-taker, liar, thief, family-protector. Or thinking about how feeling cut-up crazy was better than feeling bad and dirty. There were no nightmares that night; in fact I had no trouble falling asleep at all. My first thought the next morning was how to get more alcohol.

We lived in a nice area close to the waterfront, but a few blocks down and around the corner were some brick row houses where several bootleggers did their business. I knew they were there because my father, who was a policeman, called them "scourges." I'd heard him telling Mom how he'd seen customers leaving with their purchases in a brown paper bag after paying the "godawful price of seventy-five cents for a bottle of Westminster Sherry."

Desperate to feel the way I had at the party, I decided to go to the bootlegger myself. I listed what I would need, folded the paper carefully, and hid it in a washed-out Avon perfume pot, a favourite hiding-place. Before everyone was up the next morning, I collected what I needed and hid it outside.

That night after supper, when it was dark, I put on my disguise in the alleyway behind our house: one of Mother's hats, the brim low on my forehead, her reading glasses, and her old forest-green cloth coat that she hadn't worn for years. Shaking in her black, high-heeled rain boots with the zippers on the side, I climbed the cracked cement steps to the bootlegger and thumped the door three times. A young man not much older than me opened it.

"One bottle of Westminster Sherry," I said, and dropped three twenty-five-cent pieces in his hand. "And don't forget the paper bag," I said in the gruff voice I'd rehearsed. He disappeared and returned in a flash, thrust the bag at me, and slammed the door. I thought I was going to faint. Not from fear, but from relief. No more nightmares or lying awake wishing I were dead.

In the laneway behind my house I peeled off my disguise and sank down on my haunches against the limestone wall. I unscrewed the cap, tipped up the bottle with one hand, and pinched my nose closed with the other the way Mom did with bitter medicine. It tasted worse than castor oil, and smelled as bad as water left in a vase of flowers too long. I slid down the wall, stretched out my legs, and took another swig. Soon I felt warm and loose, and imagined myself standing up in a far-off place, proud and clean. I was free, free of the bad man and his stench, free of the worry about Peter and Rusty, free of the look of disapproval in Dad's eyes, the confusion in Mom's.

From deep in my wine-warmed gut, a sound escaped that haunted me for weeks: a half-laugh rife with pain, trying to be something it wasn't. It reminded me of Aunt Ruby's cackle, a worn-out, weary-of-life sound.

§

Although I'd lost some weight, I was still heavier than my friends, and I didn't want to go to the Grade Eight graduation dance. I'd seen a fat girl in a prom dress once and she looked like an elephant in a tutu. I wanted to try to fit in, though, just this once. Ralph Babcock asked me to go with him, but he was fat too. Mom said that Mrs. Etmansky, her dressmaker, would make me a dress. "We'll find shoes and a purse to dye the exact colour. You'll look beautiful," Mom told me. I didn't think my mother ever lied, but that day I knew she did.

The fittings made me want to throw up. I hated the way the dress fell just below my knees and revealed how one leg was thinner than the other one and connected to a deformed ankle and instep, thick and humped-up over the side of my shoe. At my last fitting, looking into the mirror with disgust, I remembered my friend Michael's silver flask and how I forgot that night how ugly I was.

Ralph came to the house in a navy blue suit, the buttons straining the buttonholes. Dad made silly jokes. Mom put out a plate of hors d'oeuvres: crackers and cheese, homemade pickles stuck with toothpicks waving multi-coloured cellophane flags, Coca-Cola in her best glasses. Pictures were taken, which I'd tear up as soon as I had the chance. We sat in the front room, stiff and nervous as robots needing oil. I pretended I didn't pinch. Ralph pretended to like me. My parents pretended I was a normal young girl, thrilled about her first prom.

I didn't care. I felt the amber liquid I'd stolen from my father's bottle swish-swishing in the washed-out horseradish jar I'd put in the aqua purse that matched my dress and shoes. Ralph was shocked when I pulled out the bottle on the way up the hill, but he got over that after his first sip. I swallowed and waited. The bad, dirty girl dropped away like a blood-filled tick and was squashed under my flip-flopping aqua shoe.

That night the school gym became a luminous cloud for me to dance on, a fairy princess on shapely deer legs that arose from perfect ankles. Embroidered wings sewn with silken threads carried me over the cumulus carpet. All eyes in the room admired my tiny waist and delicate shoulders. A wreath of aqua roses braided with golden ribbons rested on my head. For one perfect night, I twirled and spun—beautiful, just as Mom said.

5 · And Again

It seemed as though he was always there, his belly flopped against the rail of his front stoop, a toothpick turning, turning between his pursed lips. I knew he was watching me, his eyebrows tense with a new wariness, and a lifetime of winters in his eyes. A skilful predator, he was sure of my silence.

But for now, thoughts of a new beginning at high school were enough to distract me. The pills had resulted in some weight loss, and I was thrilled to find that the clothes in Purdy's Young Miss Shop fit me now. Mom bought me my first crinoline—folds of cream netting edged in lace, and a smooth satin waistband—a full yellow skirt, and a white cotton blouse with an embroidered collar. I was slim enough now to tuck in my top, and I adored my belt with a silver poodle on the buckle. I wore tiny pearl studs on my newly pierced ears, and my hair was long enough to wear in a double ponytail, the latest rage. My skirt swished and crackled and I felt a little pretty, at least on the outside.

I looked forward to class, but I couldn't sit still. Many trips a day to the washroom for a cigarette, a pill, and sometimes a swig from the horseradish jar helped to muffle the sound of my fear. The roar had begun as a vague rumbling after my first night in that house, after the threats against Peter and Rusty. Gradually it had swelled to a cacophony of feelings, pressing me forward when all I wanted was to be still, to rest. I reacted to everything like a pressure cooker, the least little bump against me threatening to release a torrent of steam.

Just before Grade Ten a young girl and her family moved into the house beside Ruthie. Lily was tall and beautiful, with long, silky hair that bounced when she moved, but her front teeth were so rotten that she never smiled. She carried herself with pride, even though her father drank and sometimes fell in a heap on their front lawn. Lily read the Bible and went to church every Sunday. Sometimes when I couldn't find Ruthie, Lily was gone too, and I realized they were off together somewhere. Then Ruthie told me we couldn't be pals anymore because I swore. Didn't I know that was a sin? It felt as if I'd been thrown away like an old coat. Hurt and confused, I swallowed too many square orange pills—not intending suicide, only seeking relief from the crushing rejection.

At the hospital a doctor asked a million questions and wrote my answers in a book with a black leather cover. He nodded his head up and down, up and down, like a plastic dog stuck to the dashboard in a car. I had several more appointments with him, but I didn't tell him about the bad man. I didn't tell him about the sound. And I didn't tell him about the crack that was growing in my heart.

I remember little about Grade Ten except rattling about the school corridors in confusion, nothing in my life making sense. I worried about my parents worrying about me. My moods swung high and low, and I acted "not quite right in the head," as I'd heard Dad put it to Mom when I eavesdropped on the stairs.

One evening I heard them talking later into the night than usual. The next day Mom said, "Maybe it would be best if you went away for a while, honey. Dad and I found a boarding school in Belleville, only an hour's drive away. There's an opening for the Grade Eleven fall term. It would be good for you—new friends, interesting kids from all over the country. What do you say?"

I didn't really care where I was. I'd feel the same wherever I went. I didn't say so, but I thought it would be better for my family if I were gone.

"Isn't Belleville close to where Ruthie's moving?" I said, trying to sound enthusiastic.

"Yes, dear, just a few miles away."

"Okay, I'll go."

Just before summer ended, Ruthie and her family moved. I heard that her mother had tried to jump off their balcony the previous year, and soon after swallowed poison. I watched them drive away from the same spot they had arrived eleven years before in the big yellow truck. I remembered how excited I'd been then to have a new friend to play with. I didn't know that a sickness would come too, a sickness that spread a stain around the neighbourhood and smeared itself over so many lives.

He was still hurting Ruthie, I was sure of it. What would become of her now? Was it time to say something? But he had told me over and over that no one would believe me.

And I believed him.

§

At the beginning of September we drove up the circular drive-way to the girls' dormitory in my new school. I was wearing a scowl the size of a serving platter and I'd dyed my hair tar-black, a pitiful act of defiance, I suppose. Mom was hiding behind her denial-framed glasses, and Dad was sporting his grey felt hat with the red feather, and a navy-and-red striped tie held in place by a gold clip. His disappointment in me, that he had to bring me here at all, was fixed firmly behind a gruff-ness punctuated with silly jokes.

The dormitory, a failed attempt at modern architecture, was stuck like a drab lump between two elegant limestone build-ings. A pair of stately balsam firs stood on either side, and I imagined them feeling offended at having to stand guard on such a monstrosity. We climbed the concrete steps. My suit-cases were plunked down at the reception desk, but I held onto the cloth bag crammed with chocolate bars, three horseradish jars of Westminster Sherry, and a few packages of non-filter Player's cigarettes.

The residence matron was a stocky woman with blotchy skin who trailed a tobacco smell. She pointed at two narrow beds, two desks, two night tables, and two lamps in my room. A small washroom with a sink and toilet was off to the left of the doorway, and the showers were down the hall, she said.

"And this is your roommate, Margaret. Margaret, this is Nancy."

The girl sitting on the bed looked shockingly like Ruthie. She smiled grimly but didn't say anything. And I resigned myself, for my parents' sake.

The location had changed, but my feeling-life hadn't, and I missed my home more than I let on. I called Mom and Dad on weekends, but failed to mention I was usually grounded for breaking some idiotic rule, of which there were many. I thought it was unfair that the boys were allowed to smoke in their common room but the girls weren't, so I found numerous cubbyholes in our dormitory to smoke in. Each time the matron smelled smoke, she scurried around, nose twitching, trying to discover the offender. She scooted and sniffed till the end of the school year like a human smoke detector, zigzagging through the halls, peeking in broom closets and stairwells.

Mom sent my pills from Kingston every month, but they didn't seem to work as they had before. My ravenous appetite was back, I couldn't stop thinking about *him* and the dreadful things I'd done, and I worried about Ruthie. She hadn't returned my phone calls. At a routine doctor's appointment I asked for another prescription for the same pills. Outside the drugstore, I swallowed three without water. I arrived back at school buzzing with energy and could barely remember why I'd been so upset.

I loved the classes, but my favourite time of day was the evening, from seven to nine, in the study hall, a classroom off the downstairs hallway. It seemed a quiet, peaceful place, set apart from the commotion inside of me. I often pictured myself living in the worlds of *Hamlet* or *Wuthering Heights*. Through the windows and over the lawn and highway, I could see the harbour lights twinkling like tiny shore-stars. Still, it was difficult to focus or sit still for long periods of time, and I'd often slip out for a cigarette.

§

My parents came to visit, Mom carrying a box of homemade treats, including a whole Queen Anne cake with sticky icing dribbled on top, just the way I liked it. She looked rested and elegant in her feather hat and the tweed walking-suit we'd picked out together at Sears, and seemed glad to see me. That look was gone from Dad's face, which made me so happy that I cried when we hugged hello.

We decided to go for a drive, and I was allowed to smoke in front of my parents for the first time. When they asked me where I wanted to go, I suggested visiting Ruthie. She and her family had moved to a village not far away.

We arrived at a rundown general store her parents had purchased. It looked eerily out of place in the tidy town, like a tumbledown shack in an old western movie. I wondered why I felt numb about seeing the bad man again.

"Ruthie isn't feeling well," said her mother, even more hunched and black-circled around the eyes. But she waved to the stairs anyway, with a limp flick. I climbed the narrow steps and turned the corner. The door was open halfway. Ruthie's room was dim and smelled like her father. I felt a greasy hand from the past swipe across my senses, and I leaned against the doorframe for support.

"Ruthie, it's Nancy. I came from school for a visit. Can I come in?"

"Yes, come in," she said, sounding a thousand years old and far away, like a bad phone connection.

What I saw haunts me still. Ruthie was curled up in a fetal position on her side. Her eyes were hollow-old. Her curly raven hair was matted and stuck to her head, as if it had just given up.

"What's the matter, Ruthie? Are you sick?"

"No, I'll be fine," she said, her mouth barely moving. She brushed her hand at the air dismissively, as if all those years squashed like a bug under that despicable man were nothing. "I just need some rest. You'd better go now."

"Are you sure? Can I get you anything? Why didn't you call me back? I was worried."

"No," she said, her voice agitated, "I'll be fine. I'm just tired. I can't talk to you right now. Please! Just go."

"Well, okay. Call me at school. Bye, Ruthie," I said, my voice sounding much like hers.

I knew that we had been mauled by the same madness, that what ailed her wouldn't respond to rest. I didn't know that she'd forgotten it all to protect herself. I didn't know that in her mind she was, even as we spoke, somewhere else, a kinder, safer place. On the way downstairs I realized that she had it too—a crack the size of a man, right through her heart, a gouge so full of shame and guilt and despair that there was no room for love to get in or out.

I was so mad at her and him and everyone that I wanted to scream, "What's the matter with all you people? Can't anyone see the bruise on Ruthie, the bruise the shape of *him*?"

When I reached the bottom of the stairs I saw him standing behind the counter. He barely raised his head, but his eyes moved like a devil's, sure that he still had my soul. He snaked his almost-smile, that slippery, smirking, knowing smile, across the room. I felt his eyes travel my body as if he still owned me.

I wanted to kill him right there, in front of the jars of candy that I was sure he was still using for bait. I wanted to make a crack in his heart too. I wanted to tear out that horrid thing that lived under his still-dirty shirt, that demanding, ruthless worm waiting like a poisonous eel to strike at anything handy and vulnerable. The look on my face must have spoken for all the years he stole from me. It must have revealed the murder in my mind. He lowered his head and pretended to be busy. I knew he could see that I remembered well.

§

Just before the school year ended, I injured my shoulder when I was practising on the trampoline in the gym. The pain was so severe it was difficult not to cry. One of the staff (I'll call him Mr. Grant, but that's not his real name) helped me into the car and drove me to the hospital. He seemed kind and gentle, patting me on the knee to assure me I was in good hands, that everything would be all right. I'd never felt such pain before and lost consciousness on the way. At the hospital the doctor said I'd dislocated my shoulder.

I was given medication that made me dizzy and sleepy. My arm was strapped to my chest. The doctor said I could rest for a while and go back to school when I was ready. Mr. Grant stayed with me. My eyes were heavy. I heard the door handle rattling as if someone were checking to see if it locked.

I was so tired.

Then I felt him touching me. His mouth twisted and his eyes glazed, and his hands were busy with both of us. "You like it, don't you. You like it," he said, over and over and over, a cruel mantra I'll never forget.

I think I believed him. That was the only possible explanation for this happening to me again. That day, in that bright-white room, a steel strand of shame tightened around my heart and squeezed off another piece. Somehow he'd known he could get away with it. He'd known I believed that I deserved it.

I pretended for a while that everything was fine, that I didn't need that piece of myself that he had dropped like a dirty Kleenex on the hospital floor. But that didn't work. It was all I thought about for the next two weeks. The convocation picture that hangs in the school hall captured my misery perfectly: swollen eyes that couldn't look up for the photographer, mouth pulled tight over clenched teeth, slumped old-woman shoulders.

I couldn't sleep. A frantic jig danced in my head. What was wrong with me? How did the bad men find me? Did they smell my shame? Could they pick up something about me that alerted them to my being easy prey? Maybe they noticed my foot that didn't look quite right and made assumptions.

That frightened me. I couldn't stop thinking about who else would notice the signs and pick me off like a duck in a carnival shooting gallery. They would have to be sly observers, their eyes constantly panning for that look or gesture that revealed that I was already soiled, that another bit of dirt wouldn't matter. I began to glance furtively behind me as I walked between the school and my dorm, suspecting that the other teachers were peering at me, seeking out my chink. I stopped wearing makeup and doing my hair. Maybe if made myself even uglier they wouldn't notice I was damaged goods.

Maybe if I got fat again, I wouldn't be noticed.

§

School was over. Driving home with my parents, I tried to be excited that summer had come. I practised forgetting, and thought of how it always tickled me to be in our car, a yellow and white 1956 Plymouth station wagon. It reminded me of a jumbo metal smile, expansive and carefree with its pointy, silver fins.

At the last-day tea, the teachers had told my parents about the ribbons I'd won in shot put at the track meet. My marks weren't bad, they'd said, considering that I hadn't been able to use my arm for six weeks. My father beamed. My mother smiled her usual "I knew she could do it."

I wanted to tell them everything. That Ruthie was dying under that horrible man, that I needed to do *something* so that the bad men wouldn't notice me, that I felt as though I was cracking inside and I thought I'd die. But I couldn't. They were happy and I felt it was up to me to keep them that way. On the way home I cradled my broken heart in my lap and resigned myself to there always being a bad man.

§

My parents said I could return to my old high school the next fall for Grade Twelve. That summer I had corrective surgery on my polio foot—a wedge of bone was removed and redistributed —and I recuperated at the cottage with my leg in a cast.

It was one of those days that nature, out of sheer mischief, could convince anyone was a day for fun. The wind played with the water, coaxing it into curls, with a touch of froth on top. Our steel boat reflected the sun in a thousand flashing ricochets. Dragonflies darted back and forth through the perfect summer air, their diaphanous wings brilliant in purple and bottle-green. My foot would look so much better, the doctor said. The dragging and the flip-flop would be barely noticeable. I couldn't wait to get the cast off.

Mom and Dad had gone for a drive and left Peter in charge of me. He had put together a pair of water skis from a kit and was waxing them with reverent strokes. I was daydreaming about a pair of high heels to go with my new foot.

One of the few things I did well was water ski. Peter and I were both fearless on the water, jumping the wake and slapping the water with such a crack it could be heard clear across the lake. Mom, always a good sport, drove the boat, although I knew she worried we were too reckless.

When I complained about how much I missed skiing, Peter's face changed into that angel-scamp grin that always meant fun. "I have an idea."

We wrapped my leg, cast and all, in a garbage bag and secured it with duct tape. Then he helped me onto the edge of the dock, one foot in a ski and the other in the bag. I couldn't wait to hit the water.

At the wheel of the boat, Peter gave a signal. The engine roared and I was up and flying. Laughing and hooting, I swung back and forth across the wake, curving the ski just so, and producing a ten-foot arc of water behind me. Peter's grin grew wider and wider. We wove our way down the lake and zoomed past the dock of my parents' friends. We thought we were pretty clever. One of the people on the dock began to stab the air with his arm, pointing back to where we'd come from. It was then that I realized that the man was my father and the woman next to him with a face of stone was Mom.

Peter turned the boat homeward. Unfortunately we hadn't thought ahead. I realized that in order to get out of the water I'd have to let go of the ski rope and drop into the water. The plaster cast would turn to mush.

The dock between our cottage and the one next door slanted into the water. If I timed it just right, I could drop the ski rope and glide up onto the dock. And I'd end up standing —I hoped. I let go, cut through the water, and slid up the ramp, slippery with moss. For a moment I teetered, then fell on my backside—but I kept my bagged leg in the air.

Peter's face was worried as he helped me up. My dry landing may have helped his case a little, but we caught hell that day. Still, we laughed in secret at how clever we'd been.

That was the best summer I ever had. The surgery was a success, so that if I held my foot just so (after a great deal of practice in front of the long mirror in my parents' bedroom), the dragging-flipping motion disappeared.

My weight continued to drop. The candy was, for the most part, replaced by regular sips from the horseradish jar. Only occasionally did I seek comfort in sweets, when the sound of my feelings, that insufferable roar, became a vortex around me.

The next year began slowly and easily, then burst into a whirlwind. It convinced me in its utter treachery that I was beautiful, that I'd found a place to fit. It lifted me to the realms of womanhood, blinded me to reality, and plugged my ears to the truth. And it set me down in a place that falsely promised I'd be loved and taken care of.

One Saturday afternoon a fellow I was dating took me to a dance club I'd heard much about. We sat at a small table in a dim cavern that sizzled with intrigue and adventure. My friend introduced me to Mack, the owner, who also operated a dance studio and an after-hours coffeehouse. When my friend went to the bar for our drinks, Mack came over in his snazzy velvet smoking jacket, pipe in hand, moving so smoothly he appeared to be on wheels. He sat down and began to light his pipe ever so slowly, his eyes burning on my face. "Why don't you come back tomorrow night—by yourself," he said. I was flabbergasted but tried not to show it.

The next evening he met me at the door, put his arm around my shoulder in a protective way, and ushered me to the bar. The smell of beer, smoke, and sweat was titillating, and I'd never seen so many liquor bottles all in one place. I noticed everyone staring at us. "What's your pleasure, my dear?" he said, cocking his head as though my answer would mean the world to him.

"Rum and Coke, no ice," I said. We stood drinking at the bar and before long I felt feathery, as though I could float off. He showed me to a table, his hand gently pressing my back. When he pulled the chair out for me, I felt like royalty. He asked me many questions, particularly about my relationship with my family, and listened intently to my answers.

We danced to music I'd never heard before, music so bewitching that my legs noodled, my skin prickled, my pulse thumped in my ear. I fell in love with the throbbing beat, and the way it felt to be a somebody. I couldn't stay away.

A few weeks later, Mack asked me if I'd like to learn to dance, Latin American style—mambo, tango, cha-cha, rumba, and samba.

"When you're ready, you could teach at my dance studio," he said. "But you'd have to work the bar Wednesday, Friday, and Saturday night at the club." I'd never been so flattered. .

"I don't know," I said regretfully. "My father would have a fit."

"You're a grown woman now, aren't you? You can do whatever you want, can't you?"

"Well, it's just that my father ... "

"You don't have to worry about a thing," he interrupted. "*I'll* be looking after you from now on. Come to the studio Saturday morning. Ten sharp."

In my last year of high school I spent most evenings at the club. Working behind the bar and teaching dance classes gave me a wonderful sense of belonging, as well as the opportunity to drink an incredible amount of rum and Coke. It also added one more nick to the crack in my heart. My dad, after all, was a policeman. Breaking the law by serving minors, as a minor, didn't feel good or right. But I didn't want to upset Mack, either. He frightened me when he was angry.

Mack wasn't bad looking. He thought he was gorgeous. He said he was five-foot-eleven, but I knew he wasn't because I was five-foot-ten and he was my height in his bare feet. His skin was light brown with a touch of gold, as if there was a light on underneath. Every Saturday night he yanked out his nose hairs and trimmed his muttonchops. He lifted weights and spent a good deal of time staring in the mirror flexing his muscles. His pants were tailored tight as could be, and his shoes were spit-polished till they gleamed. People called him the Shadow.

He had a slight stutter, which was more obvious when he was angry. The threat of his violent temper kept his staff under his thumb—where he seemed to like his adoring entourage to be. Everything about him was contrived to produce an effect. The way he fondled his pipe and held his head a little too high were all designed to trick the observer. He didn't want people to think I was too friendly or "common," and instructed me not to smile, but to be aloof, so that men at the club wouldn't approach me.

He came from Eastern Canada, and his humble beginnings, I later realized, had infected him with an enormous sense of entitlement. He had a reputation for being viciously jealous, but I was swept away by his attention and couldn't see the danger.

Dad hated him. He frequently explained the dangers of the situation to me, and forbade me to see Mack. My disobedience infuriated him. When he spoke about Mack, he thumped his fist on any handy surface, his face reddened, and the veins in his temples throbbed. That worried me, not for myself but for him.

The drinking age was twenty-one then. The city bylaws stated that no liquor was to be served in local bars. Hard liquor licences could be obtained only for private establishments. Somehow, through his connections, Mack was able to get a private licence for his club. He brought in rhythm-and-blues bands from Montreal, and sometimes there was a line-up all the way around the block. The availability of hard liquor was enticing, and the thumping, grinding atmosphere was a novelty back then.

City officials had created a police unit called the morality squad that would make regular visits to any place alcohol was served to ensure that drinking laws were upheld. Most of the clientele at Mack's club were under age. Dad said that Mack chose me in order to deter the squad from raiding the club. They'd have to arrest me along with everyone else, which, because of Dad's position, would have been an embarrassment. He said it was obvious to everyone but me that I was this man's protection from the law. My father said Mack was manipulating the police, with me as his unwitting accomplice. I know now that he was right, but I didn't believe him then. I thought Mack loved me.

§

My parents bought a piece of land for their retirement home on Devil Lake. Dad's parents had worked as tenant farmers on the property in the late 1800s and early 1900s. Now it was valuable lakeshore real estate, and the owner wouldn't sell it to just anyone, although he'd had many offers. Mr. Tett, who was in his eighties, was the man Dad's parents had worked for. That Dad had been successful enough to be able to make an offer to the man his parents had worked for was a big deal. He and Mom were thrilled when the purchase was completed, and they invited me to visit the land with them early in the new year.

The day before we went, Dad bought me a white fake-fur winter coat with a black stripe around the edge of the hood. He disdained fussing about clothes, and I was deeply moved that he'd picked it out all by himself. It was the most beautiful coat I'd ever seen. After modelling it for my folks, I ran up the back stairs and buried my face in the soft material. I wished I could still tell Dad everything, the way I did when I was a little girl. I agreed to go with them, and I wore the coat.

We walked the perimeter of the property as Dad shared his plans, pointing excitedly, and forgot for a brief time the tension between us. Mom nodded her head, smiling the way mothers do when their nest appears to be in order. Dad said that his parents had died working this land for someone else. It was clear that the memory was difficult, for his eyes floated in watery pools of the past.

The snow lay like velvet on this land that he loved—it lay on the tips of the branches like mittens, on fence posts like toques. We walked the shoreline and Dad pointed to an island about half a mile down the lake. In his twenties, he said, he'd carried supplies across the lake on a makeshift barge, then up the hill, to build a cottage for the Vanderbilt family, who summered there.

Mack had forbidden me to go with them. When I phoned and told him I'd gone with my parents he was incensed. The next time we met he yanked the coat off my back. "You disobeyed me," he snarled. "I told you not to go. Now get out of here, and don't come back until you've told your father you gave me the coat."

I had to walk home from the club in the cold, coatless. There was something dark and cruel and unsettling about Mack's behaviour. Could Dad be right? The thought slid off me, though, the way all painful things did back then, and slipped into the crack.

When Dad noticed the coat missing from the hall closet, I said that someone had stolen it from the club. A few days later Dad saw Mack on the street wearing the coat. I could tell he was hurt, but I didn't know how to soothe him. What I *did* know was that I didn't dare say anything to Mack for fear of his temper. I also knew that hurting Dad by showing him where my loyalties lay was exactly what Mack had intended.

§

My father and I reached a crossroads on a blazing-hot June day, in front of a limestone cathedral rich with tradition.

Dad was coming home from the police station for lunch. I was on my way to teach a cha-cha lesson at the club on my school lunch hour. Noticing Dad before he saw me, I felt a tug in my chest. He always carried himself like a king, and looked every bit the part in his uniform and gleaming black boots. He raised his head but didn't smile, for he knew where I was going.

He slowed down, his chin quivering, his face solemn.

"Come home with me, Nancy. Please! That man'll be the death of you." His voice shook. He removed his policeman's cap and wiped his brow with the back of his hand. "Please listen to me, just this once."

"I'll be late for the lesson, Dad. I'll see you at supper." I was sweating too. I'd run out of my orange pills two days before and badly needed to pick them up at the drugstore before the lesson.

"Nancy-girl, please," he said, his tears right on the brim. "That man is just using you. What's the matter with your head?"

He hadn't called me Nancy-girl for a long time. It made me want to bury my head in the soft hollow in his neck and tell him how my boyfriend was mean sometimes, how I was worried sick about all the pills I was taking but couldn't seem to do without. I wanted to tell him how much I loved him, how I didn't mean to be such a terrible daughter but couldn't help myself. The words wouldn't come. They were choked by need. I had to get to the drugstore.

"Tell Mom I'll be home for supper," I said as I turned my back to him. I walked half a block but was compelled to turn around. I wish I hadn't. What I saw became part of the roar. My tall, proud father was crying like a child, stooped and broken, his face in his hands.

That day in front of the cathedral I suddenly recognized how vast the wall was that had been building up between us. A wall so long and wide and high we could never have been able to reach over it to speak to one another.

Words would have smashed the wall, would have brought down the blocks piled high with assumptions, pride, and shame. He thought I had chosen a life that made a mockery of his duties as a policeman. He changed toward me. He never again looked directly at me, as if afraid it might remind him of that thieving day. I thought he hated me, had finally found out what a horrid person I really was.

My mountain, the safest place I ever knew, became an ache, a longing, a locked box. Late into the night, hoping to find the key, I'd write poems to him that he never saw. Words would have opened the box, but neither of us could speak them, even if we had known what they were.

He must have felt we were on different sides, that I was an enemy of his heart. Neither of us knew that a disease had me in its clutches, that it was rolling me into a ball, moulding my choices and decisions.

The bells of the cathedral rang twelve times. They would toll for forty years with the image of my father sobbing on the street. They would toll for a father who thought he had been forsaken. He went to a place fathers go when it hurts too much to love.

I went to the drugstore.

§

A year after I met Mack I found myself pregnant. When the doctor gave me the news, he smirked, his eyes familiar. Resigned, I accepted the shame as his words slid smoothly into the ever-widening crack. This is what happened to bad girls. I'd heard it a hundred times.

Abortion was illegal back then. Mack arranged one anyway with a gynecologist who I later learned was an underground advocate of women's rights. I went to his office on the way to an algebra exam. He explained the procedure, punctured my placenta with the longest needle I'd ever seen, and gave me some pills to induce the abortion.

"Come straight back to my office after your exam," he said. "I want to be able to check on you until it's over. It's important that you do as I ask."

After my exam, I began to walk the ten blocks home. I saw no reason to go back to the doctor's office. Abuse had taught me to disconnect from my body, so I ignored the scraping pain until it seemed only a vague gnawing. We lived close to the university, a neighbourhood that had slowly changed to a student rental area and lost its pristine small-town look. The untended lawns were strewn with bicycles, and leaning garbage cans spilled over with waste. "Going to hell in a handbasket," Mom would say. I increased my pace. A nearly full bottle of pills was wrapped in my underwear at the back of my dresser drawer.

When I got home I started to cramp. Large blobs like crimson globules in a lava lamp slid into the toilet bowl. I didn't remember anything else.

My parents were in Florida on vacation. My brother, still in university, had married and lived across the street. Aunt Ruby lived with us in a room upstairs, where she cooked on a hot plate. About the only time we ever saw her was when she came down for the occasional supper when my parents were home.

She found me lying unconscious in the downstairs washroom. Mom and Dad were called back from Florida. The doctor said I'd lost a lot of blood, and that lying on the floor for so long before I'd been discovered hadn't helped matters. I suppose I was lucky, but I just wanted to be left alone.

The doctors and nurses, all with grave faces, urged me to tell them who had done did this thing. "You're lucky to be alive," they told me, expecting me to be happy about it.

Mom, crying endless tears of anger and relief, tugged at my bed sheets and smoothed my pillows. Dad's tears were the dry kind that made him mix up his words so they didn't come out right. His helpless rage must have made it difficult for him, but he resisted saying "I told you so."

The day before I was discharged from the hospital I heard a kerfuffle in the hall outside my hospital room, and leaned forward in the bed to look. Dad was yanking his arm away from Mom so that his coat pulled off his shoulder.

"I'll kill the son of a bitch," Dad said, yanking his coat back up.

"Don't do it, Orville, don't go."

"For Christ's sake, Carmel, she nearly died in there."

"She's coming around. The doctor said so. Come home, dear. We'll talk there."

Mom had brought my purse to the hospital. While I was unconscious and the blood transfusion drip-dripped, she must have looked inside. Having discovered the dark poetry that revealed my ambivalence about life, she arranged for a psychiatrist to see me. Future appointments were arranged. The hospital staff continued to try to persuade me to reveal who had performed the abortion. But I needed to get home. A box of stale chocolates from Christmas and a horseradish jar of sherry were hidden along with the pills.

At home I phoned Mack, and we arranged to meet at the club. He wrapped his arms around me when I got to the top of the stairs, then led me to a chair. He'd brought a pillow from his apartment for me to sit on. He pulled his chair close to mine and handed me a rum and Coke.

"I was worried about you," he said. "You should have gone back to the doctor's office as you were told. Before you do *anything* from now on, you must check with me first."

Flattered by his possessiveness and convinced I needed to be kept in line, I allowed Mack to control my every move. Looking back, I understand that I had simply exchanged the sexual abuse for another kind. My acceptance of the violence in our relationship showed how little I valued myself. And I was used to living in fear. It was what people like me knew with a chilling certainty. was their lot in life.

I went back to Mack, pretending he was kind and knew what was best for me. I went back to chewing, sipping, and swallowing until my tongue was raw and my body was numb. My parents went back to pretending this ugly thing hadn't happened and swept it under the bulging familial carpet. What else could they do?

§

When a bylaw was passed that allowed the local bars to serve liquor as well as beer and wine, Mack's club no longer had a monopoly on liquor sales. Social preferences for a night on the town changed, and his business went downhill. He owed a lot of money, and often used my ten-dollar allowance to buy stock for the bar. Eventually we left for Toronto, sneaking off in the middle of the night. Driving there in the pounding rain, I was aware of a hole inside me the size of my dreams for a university education.

I hoped the sound wouldn't follow me. But it did, a slithering thing that made its nest and waited. I didn't know that the road to Toronto pointed to hell. But it did, as surely as if it were a finger on the bad man's hand. I knew I should stop the car and run for my life, but my legs were governed by the certainty that I deserved no better.

For the first few weeks we stayed in a rooming house in Cabbagetown, around the corner from Mack's brother. We had little money, so we made bologna and mustard sandwiches, and drank orange juice from cartons that also held the window open. The city's breath, sticky and heavy with heat, wrapped itself around my body.

In that cramped, dreary room, confused and homesick, I realized with blistering clarity that I didn't love Mack. It was only decades later that I understood fully my compulsion to punish myself by choosing relationships that would confirm my own worthlessness, as if I were a quality-control inspector whose job it was to stamp "substandard" on myself over and over again.

Trying to sound cheerful, I called Mom to tell her of my plans to find work. She said, in the tender, calm voice that mothers save for runaway daughters, "Come on home, honey. Dad'll come around. Everything'll be all right."

My knees buckled. I would have given anything to be pin-curling her hair and giggling over tea. "Don't worry, I'll be okay," I said. "I'll call soon. I love you."

I hated Toronto. The constant clanking of construction equipment, the clanging of trolley cars, and the impatient honking of car horns cast a spell of relentless busyness over the city. A million voices thrummed in the air as hurrying bodies heaved themselves onto buses and subway cars.

A letter arrived from Mom. She wrote cheerfully about canning tomatoes, and said that a whippoorwill's nattering outside her window just after dawn was driving her crazy.

She planned to put up a sign that said, "No singing before 8:00 AM."

I laughed out loud, a hollow, lonesome sound. Mom had an endearing sense of humour, innocent and sweet. I choked back the tears, longing to be standing next to her at the sink, looking down Devil Lake while we cleaned tomatoes. There was a twenty-dollar bill for a bus ticket in the envelope. Before Mack could see the money, I hid it and made an appointment with a doctor. Soon I had a bottle of square orange pills, and the gnawing homesickness faded, along with the disturbing notion that I'd made a grievous mistake by coming here with Mack.

I was hired for eighty-five dollars a week by Precision Data Cards to sell data processing supplies and printer ribbons over the phone. Mack was offered a position as a fitness instructor at a golf and country club forty miles away. He rented a room near there, and I took a tiny apartment on Hazelton Avenue in Yorkville, a short walk from my work. It was a compact cave, sparsely decorated with done-in furniture and yellowed, greasy pictures askew on the walls.

Mack usually visited on weekends, but sometimes made surprise visits late at night. He made it clear that my getting fat would be unforgivable, and would check my refrigerator frequently, throwing out anything he considered fattening. He needed me blonde, obedient, and very, very thin.

The abuse had been psychological up till now, except for some pushing, shoving, and yanking. One night when he came to my apartment I wasn't there. I'd stopped after work to have a drink with a girlfriend. When I came home I tried to explain, but he shoved me against the wall with his hand around my throat. With his other fist he jabbed me several times on the side of the head. I slid down the wall into a heap of resignation. I should have asked his permission, I told myself. Outside my apartment the neighbourhood buzzed. Folk music drifted in the window from nearby coffeehouses. As I lay beside Mack, shocked and bruised, I pictured the "free love" signs posted on hydro poles and the free spirits that milled about the crowded streets in miniskirts and thin cotton shirts and multi-coloured beads, and I was painfully, glaringly aware that I was trapped.

§

I needed more pills to counteract the tolerance I'd developed, so I used my lunch hours to seek out new doctors. The Dexedrine prevented me from sleeping, and I began to hallucinate. Shadows skulking along the walls metamorphosed into sinister human shapes sent by Mack to spy on me. I was tormented by rustlings in the closet and insinuations from the toaster.

After consulting the *Pharmaceutical Compendium* at the library, I concluded that my lack of sleep had triggered an amphetamine psychosis. So I added barbiturates to my collection of little coloured lies, and I would wash the concoction down with a few drinks. Finally I would get to sleep. Often I'd wake up to find myself rummaging through drawers and closets. It would take me thirty-six years to find what I was looking for.

Eventually I had prescriptions from over a dozen doctors. The information was difficult to keep straight, so I made lists in columns: doctor's name, type of pill, pharmacy, day the prescription was to be picked up.

One day at a pharmacy a few blocks from home I handed over a prescription. I'd forgotten that I'd left one there a few days before for the same kind of pills, from a different doctor. When the pharmacist realized what was going on, he bolted from behind the counter. "You're an addict," he screeched at me. "You're a drug addict!"

Not a common word back then, "addict" had a vile connotation. A few years before, I'd seen the movie *The Man with the Golden Arm*, a vivid depiction of heroin abuse. The scenes flashed through my mind.

"Addict! Addict!" he shouted as he chased me outside, waving the prescription in the air. Terrified, stumbling into pedestrians and garbage cans, I headed for my cave. I'll never forget slumping against my door, his words still trampling me with shame.

After the pills and the alcohol, there wasn't much money left. I began stealing food from a Dominion Store a block from my apartment. One day, on my lunch hour, I slipped a package of luncheon meat and a loaf of bread into my purse, then paid for a tube of toothpaste at the checkout. When I reached the sidewalk, I felt a hand on my shoulder. A voice said, "I need to look in your bag. Open up."

Shaking in my red and navy platform shoes, I opened my purse and exposed the stolen merchandise. The man held my arm in a vice grip and said, "Come with me. I'm calling the police."

I thought of running, but was oddly relieved that I'd been caught. When the police came, I wouldn't tell them my name, worried that my father would find out. At the station they asked me my name again. I refused to tell them. They took my purse and put me in a room with three scantily clad women. The room was grey-bare and smelled like a toilet. I'm sure my fear reeked too. I desperately hoped they wouldn't take my pills.

The sound was gnawing at me, a promise of unbearable pain. Ever since its birth in those dark rooms in the house across the street from my childhood home, I had believed that its roar would kill me if I allowed myself to hear it in all its fullness. Now it was back. Shame and pain, guilt and fear, and waves of self-loathing rolled over me in one heart-cracking surge. The room tilted. I slid to the floor and settled there, at one with the spit and the urine and the dried-up vomit.

When the policeman came to get me, he told me he'd checked my identification to see if I had a record. I told them my father was a policeman and would be devastated if he found out. I pleaded. They let me go.

Six months later, Mack moved us into an apartment north of St. Clair and Yonge. He kept the room near his job but came home on weekends. I sensed he was cheating on me, but I didn't dare mention it. Instead I continued to drink and use pills, anything but face the truth of my life. Often I had to call a taxi company when I woke up to find out what day it was.

Eventually, after confusing a workday with the weekend and missing two days of work without calling in, I was fired.

I managed to find a job as a personnel consultant, and for the first few weeks I threw myself into it. But the effort to silence my feelings soon overrode any eagerness I had to feel useful and earn a living. I lasted in that job for about six weeks, then found another.

Each job was the same. My work performance would slide, and a look of confusion and disappointment would appear on the faces of my employers. When I saw that, I would quit before they said the words. The look was the same as the one I saw on my father's face, and the same as the one reflected in my mirror.

Those were desperate times. I was either punishing myself with substances or being punished by an angry man. When Mack suggested we take karate lessons, I was glad to have found an excuse for the bruises. He frequently punched me in the head, eventually causing some hearing loss in one ear. He dragged me along the floor by my hair. But it was his brain-washing that had the most cruel and lasting effect. All that mattered to him was what was on the outside. As long as I was slim, I was an acceptable human being. I learned my lessons well. I swallowed literally thousands of the square orange pills that kept my appetite in check and the roar at bay.

In 1970 I married him.

My parents, my brother, my sister-in law, and a few of Mack's friends came to the church and the reception. I wore a white eyelet lace suit with tiny blue embroidered flowers. Dad wore his best grey suit, which closely matched the colour of his skin, and Mom wore a two-piece teal blue suit and smiled as best she could.

The church ceremony was simple and short. The only time my father spoke his true feelings was when he didn't say a word. When the minister asked if there was anyone who knew any reason that the bride and groom should not be joined, Dad noisily cleared his throat. He could see the truth of Mack. The face he put on for Mom's and my sake looked like a mask held on by sheer will. Mom was pleasant and warm, safely tucked into her place of denial, where mothers go when they can't bear the choices of their young.

Our apartment was very 1970s, wallpapered in royal blue, orange, and black polka dots. A huge orange circle was painted on the black ceiling. We had prepared the reception buffet ourselves, and there was plenty of alcohol to supply the counterfeit cheer. The picture of us cutting the wedding cake portrayed a beaming couple with a golden future. But the camera was unable to capture the most recent bruise, concealed under the sleeve of my suit jacket, or the fear churning in my belly.

Dad gravitated to one of Mack's friends, a game hunter who sprinkled his conversation with moose calls. To ease the tension of the day, Dad got a little drunk, and he and his new friend sat in the corner whooping all afternoon like a pair of lovesick moose. Mack was furious, but I was secretly delighted. Dad had tried his best to convince me that I was making a dreadful mistake, but he finally gave up when I assured him I was happy. I felt he deserved a medal for coming all that way to hand over his daughter to a man he despised.

Mack's boss, a celebrity in the fitness industry, came, with his wife, Vera. Tall and round, tanned and glowing, she was beautiful, in an ivory brocade suit and matching pumps. Although her smile was sparkling, I sensed a familiar desperation about her.

Mack told me on our wedding night that if I ever got fat like her he'd divorce me.

A few months later I heard that Vera had been admitted to a clinic to be treated for a most unforgivable ailment: she was fat. She was there to lose weight, Mack told me; otherwise the marriage would be over. When I went to see her, I learned that as part of her treatment she was taking the same diet pills as I was. They made her sick, she said, and she was terrified that she wouldn't be able to give her husband the thing he wanted most, a beautiful-on-the-outside wife. That day we bonded, prisoners of a common captor.

Soon after, Mack and I were invited to a posh ball at the country club. He bought me a black dress from Holt Renfrew, black and slinky-long with a cascading hood, the most beautiful gown I'd ever seen. I was so touched by his thoughtfulness that I cried. But when I read the tag on the collar, I understood the cruelty behind the gesture. It was a size nine, and Mack knew very well that I was a size eleven. He hung it in the doorway to the kitchen as a dangling promise: it would fit for the ball or there'd be hell to pay.

One night just before the event, as I sat on the couch watching Mack eat his supper, I looked at the dress waving from the door frame like a heartless black flag. I hadn't been eating. I felt faint and went into the bedroom to rest. When Mack finished eating his meal, he brought me a bowl of stewed tomatoes with a daub of butter on top. It had been heated, and tasted wonderful. I was touched by his kindness, but inside I felt a seething anger. "What is wrong with me?" I thought. "I should be grateful, shouldn't I?"

8 · X's and O's

After we were married, Mack announced that he wouldn't hit me anymore. And he didn't. But he began to make lengthy magnanimous speeches underneath which were sly insinuations that I'd failed him. His need to control every aspect of my life became more relentless, more obsessive. He decided what jobs I should apply for, what I should wear, whom I could and couldn't talk to at work. He mapped out my route to and from my job, decided where, when, and how long I was to exercise, what I was to read, and what television programs I was to watch. My only friends were those he picked himself, most of them much older women he met through his work. Feeling slightly feisty one day, I asked him if he'd ever cheated on me. He answered, in that artful way he had of making sure I understood it was my fault, that he had, but that he was "turning over a new leaf"—and if I knew what was good for me I'd better be grateful.

As time passed, Mack became something of a celebrity in the small town where he worked. He gathered quite a following. A Pied Piper of sorts, he trailed groups of breathless overweight women over the hills and through the woods on a variety of hyped-up fitness adventures. The face they saw was charming, even captivating. He appeared to take a genuine interest in them. But I knew the truth. He held them in contempt for being weak, spineless fatties.

After two consecutive social events at his workplace at which I was obviously intoxicated, Mack told me that if my drinking didn't stop, we were finished. I was tarnishing his trophy, sullying his image as a wellness guru. I drank more and more. His wife was a drunk, an unforgivable affront to a man like him. I later learned that he'd already been scouting for my replacement.

We had been together since I was in high school, but recently I'd begun to pare off the rind of dependence. When I was sober I could feel that I was in danger of letting him control the very rhythm of my breathing. On the rare occasions when he'd let me visit my folks for weekends, I'd stay sober, trying to fill my lungs on my own. But when I got back home I'd resume drinking, once more convinced that I needed Mack to breathe for me.

On one of those visits home I confided to my parents the truth of my life with Mack. They encouraged me to leave him, and offered to pay my rent for a few months. I remained sober, secretly changed jobs, and then, one day while he was at work, I moved my belongings.

I headed for my first AA meeting on a summer evening that buzzed with a sensual, throbbing rhythm. This is the city's mantra, I thought, and I began to hum along, with a rare sense of purpose. I felt like a toe tapping to its subtle beat. It felt good to make decisions for myself, although, like a prisoner who'd served a long sentence, I wasn't sure I could manage on my own.

At the meeting, people were genuine and welcoming, and it was reassuring to be in a church, snug and safe. Someone read from the Alcoholics Anonymous *Big Book*: "This program works for everyone unless you are constitutionally incapable of being honest with yourself." I hoped I wasn't one of those people.

After the meeting, a nicely dressed man approached me. He asked me how I was and listened carefully to my answers. I was not used to kindness, and his interest brought tears to my eyes. When he asked me to go for a coffee I quickly agreed.

He said he lived nearby. We stopped in front of his garage, and he pulled a bottle of vodka from the trunk of his car. He asked me if I would like to sit in the car and have a small drink to stop the shaking. A leave-right-now feeling fought for my attention, but the offer of a drink overrode my instincts. That drink was like all the others. My thirst came from the crack in my heart, and once aroused it was insatiable.

I had three drinks and then we went into his home. He had not drunk a drop. In one swift motion he shut the door, locked it, and secured the chain. My instincts bellowed, trying in vain to awaken my numbed reason. I rushed to the door, but a blow to my temple knocked me down and my head hit the floor with a hollow crack. I caught a glimpse of the man's face, which was contorted in anger. I could not understand why he was so enraged with me.

After flipping my body this way and that as if he were readying a slab of meat for butchering, he raped me. He grabbed my ears and slammed my head onto the wood floor. "This is your fault!" he said, and a long dangle of spittle flew from his mouth. "This is *all* your fault!" he shouted, as he pulled out of me and ejaculated on my face.

Holding my hair with one hand, he banged my head again and again against the floor. With the other hand he smeared his ooze over my face. He scooped it off my face and forced it up into my nose and mouth as if he was stuffing a chicken. My only victory, meagre but immensely satisfying, was to bite the end off his finger. He screamed and punched me in the face. I felt myself drift, but his words jarred me awake: "Stupid woman, stupid! Shouldn't have come! Not my fault!"

Then suddenly it was over, as if a viewer, bored with a program, had changed the channel. He got up and wiped his mouth. I lay there, stuck to the floor like ground-in dirt. He grabbed me by the collar of my blouse and jerked me up, then pulled me to the door, shoved my purse at my chest, and pushed me down the stairs. I bounced off the walls like a tumbling rock, smashing my nose on the way down. "This is all *your* fault!" he shouted after me. I believed him.

I lay at the bottom, bleeding from my nose and my torn ear. I spat out the remainder of his flesh and stumbled to my feet. Outside I hailed a cab and went back to my husband, a more familiar, dependable abuser—because that's what people like me did.

§

I left Mack for the last time in the summer of 1974. Something wise opened up inside me, and I was able to empty myself of him. My replacement moved into our newly built three-bedroom apartment at Yonge and Finch streets. The wraparound windows I'd been trained to clean just so and the wall-to-wall carpet I was instructed to vacuum every day would be handed over to his new recruit. I knew her. She was from a respectable, well-off family—that was very important to Mack—twenty years younger than him, beautiful, and suggestible, just the way he liked his recruits to be. I worried about her.

I stuffed the memories of his cruelty into the crack, using all the alcohol, food, and pills I could afford. But the one thing I wasn't able to keep there, no matter how hard I tried, was his threats. He swore he would tell my father everything private and personal I'd ever shared with him if I asked for a penny of support. I knew he could easily have afforded a few hundred dollars a month. All I wanted was what I was entitled to— nothing more, but certainly nothing less. My pleas were ignored. In head-hanging shame, I went to the welfare office and filled out the application for assistance.

I moved into a roach-infested room with a kitchenette at Bathurst and St. Clair. The apartment building was dank and dark. The tenants milled about the halls, staring with vacant eyes, and sometimes lay down there to rest. I could understand them. We were all the same, tired, defeated, waiting for the world to stop spinning so we could drop into a slot and rest, like balls on a roulette wheel.

I stretched my money by furnishing my room at the Salvation Army store—a mattress for the floor; two sheets, a pillow, and a case; a blanket, a towel, and a face cloth; some dishes and cutlery. Being alone was just fine. On the one hand, I was no longer under the control of a tyrant; on the other, I was free to throw bits of my self-respect onto the scrap heap, and free to commit slow, sweltering suicide one glass at a time.

My room's one window, three feet by five feet, was about two feet away from the brick building next door. Sometimes I played X's and O's on the bricks, drawing the imaginary lines with great care. Sometimes I counted the bricks, pretending that if I got the same number twice in a row, everything would be all right and I wouldn't die in this place. I could feel myself

slipping into insanity. Drugs and alcohol were wringing out
my mind one drawn-out squeeze at a time.

What bothered me the most was the cockroaches. I'd never
seen one up close before, and I hated them with everything in
me. I sprayed until I choked, and dreamed that they crawled
on me as I slept.

I'd asked Mack for the set of dishes my brother and sister-
in law had given us for a wedding present. I kept calling him,
and finally the dishes were left outside my door. Some of them
had been smashed, and there were pieces sticking out of the
plastic bags. Glad they hadn't been stolen, I glued them
together as if my life depended on it. I missed my family.

I drank when I could, and took endless pills until I fell asleep.
I dreamed the same dream over and over. In it my purse was
missing and with it my identification. Without it I couldn't
figure out who I was. I searched for it, but horrid monsters and
vicious circumstances kept it out of reach. I kept having this
same dream for twenty-three more years until I finally realized
what the lost purse represented. It was myself.

Occasionally I invited someone in to share a drink and
whatever else I needed from him to help me pretend that I was
beautiful.

§

Then there was no money left. The alcohol and the pills were
gone. The apartment changed into a massive cavern, with
moss that hung in scallops from the ceiling, dripping with my
blood. I threw my blanket on the floor to sop up the puddles,
convinced that if I didn't stop the dripping I'd bleed to death.
My cave was murdering me.

I climbed onto the chair, yanking and thrashing at the red-
drenched canopy. I lost my balance and fell into a pit of crawl-
ing creatures. The walls and floors had come alive. Teeming
waves of roaches as big as mice swarmed everywhere, covered
everything. I rolled up a newspaper and slapped at the savage
infestation, terrified that these beasts would devour me, but
my smacking and flailing failed to reduce their numbers.

A banging on the wall from next door interrupted my insanity and I fell onto the mattress, exhausted, my arms over my head, my feet tucked into my nightgown. As the drone of roaches and the drip, drip of blood struggled with my reason, I began to get it. I was having my first bout of delirium tremens.

My welfare cheque wouldn't come for four days. I knew what I had to do. I threw on my coat, headed for the drugstore, and helped myself to my first bottle of shaving lotion.

I vomited blood for two days, but the cockroaches vanished.

In a rare moment of clarity, I called a suicide hotline and told the truth to a faraway voice. I wanted it to stop, or I wanted it over.

The phone counsellor suggested I call the Donwoods treatment centre. I was given an interview, completed the necessary paperwork, and soon received a call that I'd been approved. A date was arranged to begin a four-week outpatient program. I was gruffly reminded that forty-eight hours of sobriety was necessary prior to the first day.

Previous withdrawals had always been painful, so much so that I would ultimately give in to the cravings. But I was so committed to extracting myself from the mess my life had become that this particular withdrawal period seemed less difficult. On the day the course was to begin I felt oddly alive, in spite of the shaking, the sweating, and the nausea. For luck I wore my favourite denim shirt, which I'd embroidered with tiny flowers. I carefully braided my hair and coiled it at the sides of my head.

There was no money for bus fare, so I borrowed a bicycle and began to pump my way to the facility. The trip was strenuous, but a curious sense of joy carried me forward, and I slipped like a phantom through the morning's misty freshness. The rattling trolleys, honking car horns, and screeching tires didn't bother me: it was life making a noise. I felt myself filling up with a peculiar soothing, smoothing sensation, like warm milk. Maybe I could get well ... just maybe.

It started to sprinkle rain. Feeding my face to the cooling drops, I imagined being gently washed in preparation for something special. Absorbed, I hit a trolley track, skidded, and fell off the bicycle onto my right arm. I was momentarily shaken, but I climbed back on the bike. Nothing could hurt me today. I was wrapped in dreams and tied up with promises to myself.

There were fifteen of us waiting in the reception area. We were introduced. Lacking the protection of our usual substances, we were stiff and self-conscious in our greetings. Then we moved to the meeting room, sat down, and were asked to share a bit about ourselves. The hope was palpable in the room, stroking, encouraging our sharing of the truth about our lives. We blurted out our fears, surprising ourselves with our honesty, loving the freedom of it. Every broken one of us beamed with new beginnings. Our commonality was reassuring, and we listened to each other's stories with earnest attention.

At lunch break I found myself in an arm-wrestling contest with a producer from the CBC. A large, robust, seemingly self-assured man whose dazzling blue eyes were flecked with wariness and pain, he reminded me of my father. I wanted to win, so I was secretly happy he wasn't easy on me. Then I heard a snap. My arm went limp, a zigzag of bone in my sleeve. His jovial face turned grey. As the room slid sideways, I threw up.

At the hospital they had to cut the sleeve of my denim shirt to get it off. In horror, I saw the scissors slice up the row of delicate flowers. My fingers flew the day that I stitched them —the very same day I decided for the last time to leave Mack. I cringed as the sleeve dropped into the wastebasket. Did that mean I'd have to go back to him?

The pain was deep and unrelenting, but soon the Demerol warmed my brain and I dropped into a numbing place, clean and dark. The x-rays revealed a hairline fracture along my upper right arm—probably from the fall on the way to the course, the doctor said—and another nasty break.

Pins were inserted in my arm. A body cast, with a steel rod inside to hold my arm out in front, prevented me from wearing anything but a floor-length muumuu and rolled-down panties. I stayed sober, except for the sleeping pills, and continued with the course. The cast was heavy and cumbersome, and getting on and off the bus was difficult. The summer heat, the weight of the plaster, and the stench of my flesh wafting up from underneath the cast were almost intolerable.

One day in the washroom I saw a course-mate taking some pills from an amber bottle. I asked her what they were and she told me they were Dexedrine, and that she had just returned from Mexico with several bottles. Apparently they could be purchased over the counter there. She swore me to secrecy, then gave me a whole bottle—one hundred reasons to suggest that the course was a mistake. I disappeared into the crack, lost again.

My arm healed, but inside I was festering. I was always teetering on the edge. Sometimes I held on, sometimes I longed to fall in. Sometimes my ember would fire up just enough to keep me sober for a few days, a few weeks. But then that insufferable sound, that rumble, that roar, would shake my resolve. I wanted to feel clean and good, but I couldn't bear the noise long enough for sobriety to gain a footing. I was dying. Most days I didn't care.

I was caught in a continuing cycle—intoxication, hangover, planning to drink, trying to stop—so I didn't notice the fever. My stomach was swelling and had become sore to the touch. After telling a friend of my symptoms, I agreed to go to the hospital. Tests revealed that gonorrhea had progressed to pelvic inflammatory disease, which resulted in damaged fallopian tubes. I would never have children, the doctor said.

The board of health insisted on contacting my partners. Not knowing the last names of some of them made me sick with shame. If only I could have told those men that all I really wanted was to be held, to be comforted. If only.

§

One Saturday afternoon months later, I met a man in a downtown bar well known for its rhythm-and-blues bands. He said he didn't drink, but came for the music. We talked for hours while I drank, and in the early evening he invited me to spend a few days at his farm in the country. He'd been smoking pot, I could smell it in the car. We were speeding west on the 401 when I saw the concrete wall coming for us. I turned away from the window just as we crashed. According to the officer who came to the hospital, the windshield shattered when the car hit the wall. Apparently I hurtled through the jagged glass, back first, soared over moving traffic, and landed on the other side of the highway.

The driver walked away from the accident with barely a scratch. I lay unconscious on the roadside.

My skull had been fractured, and the back of my head and neck was literally bashed to a pulp. My face would have been mush too if I hadn't turned away. My ankle was broken in several places, "smashed," the surgeon said. I went into surgery, where pins were inserted in my ankle. Caring for myself at home was impossible, so I was transferred to St. John's Convalescent Hospital until I graduated to a walking cast.

Peter flew from Deep River to visit me. I'll never forget seeing him from a distance as he strolled down the hall in his cowboy boots, jeans, and goofy hat. He grinned from a distance and my heart did somersaults, as it always did. He never once made me feel that I'd messed up again, and I wept when he left. Home, close to my family, was where I wanted to be. But I couldn't bear for them to see the gnawed-down stump I'd become.

The need for pain management introduced me to codeine, which provided a new kind of forgetting. If the crack opened, spewing up the past, codeine would help when alcohol wasn't available. Anything was better than facing life.

§

The insurance company settled the claim and I received a cheque for $13,000. I moved into an apartment at Don Mills and Lawrence Avenue close to a library and a shopping mall and managed to stay sober. I ordered a chocolate-brown velvet couch and chair, bookcases, and a real sheepskin carpet from the Simpson-Sears catalogue. Blazing orange floor-length curtains stretched across the balcony doors, and I waxed the hardwood floors till they gleamed. The prettiest table set I'd ever seen, wicker and sassy chrome with a thick smoked-glass top, sat in my dining room. Ceramic pots suspended from the ceiling in macramé slings trailed vines in variegated greens, and photographs of my family hung on the walls in every room. It felt like a real home.

The linen closet was stocked with fluffy towels, matching facecloths, and two extra sets of sheets. Lace sachets and fragrant soaps perfumed my drawers and closets. I'd stand in the hallway leaning against the wall, gazing on the crisp newness. Everything was going to be okay.

When I sat on the balcony watching the sunrise slip a golden mantle over the earth I murmured "Thank you, thank you" for another day of feeling clean and content. I hoped it was a new beginning.

One afternoon, empty and lonely, I felt the need to fill up with something, anything. But instead of going to a bar, I took a cab to the Humane Society. There were dozens of kittens there, but one in particular caught my eye. He sat in the corner of the cage, quiet-still, as if he'd resigned himself to no one wanting him. I named him Georgey and carried him home wrapped in a towel.

He was wiggly-warm and had the loudest purr, as if a small engine was buried beneath the white spot on his throat. He hissed and arched his back at the least affront. He wasn't very playful for a kitten, but he was happy to snuggle any chance he got. When I shifted him from couch to chair or carried him from room to room, I handled him with great care, as if he was God's grace in a black velvety coat. I loved how he made me feel tender and good.

Remembering my recent lean times, I stocked the cupboards with nutritious food, filled the fridge with vegetables, and set out a large bowl of fruit on the counter. My favourite bedtime snack was an enormous bowl of porridge swimming in milk and brown sugar. It reminded me of home. As I stirred huge pots of soup, my little friend threaded figure eights around my ankles or sat in my apron pocket. I'd loll on my gleaming brass bed while Georgey curled up on my chest like a hairy snail. I wasn't used to peace and comfort.

And the sound came, a relentless, blaring thing. It echoed off the walls, pulled down the vines, tipped the photographs into grotesque patterns. I spent the remainder of the insurance settlement at the liquor store, and my home became another cave. I hibernated for three months, swallowing, swallowing.

My foot wasn't healing well. The procedure to remove the pins had been postponed twice. After examining my foot, the doctor said he was worried about the swelling and redness that had appeared since my last appointment. An array of antibiotics had been tried, but the infection lingered. I'd read that alcohol interfered with antibiotics, and knew I had to tell the doctor about my drinking.

Sick with shame, I revealed the truth at my next appointment. "You'll lose your foot if you don't stop," he said. "I've seen it happen."

The next few months I kept sober, biding my time. I read several of Taylor Caldwell's novels, ponderous tales of humanity at its best and worst. Reading her stories gave my foot the time it needed to heal, and life trickled into me, insistently reminding me it was still there.

I polished the glass tabletop again, trimmed the vines, and waxed the floors till they shone. But most of all I stood at the mirror. Someone else had appeared there. A pleasant face with bright blue eyes looked back at me. A real smile had replaced the well-practised, glued-on one. I peered at her endlessly, wondering who she was, hoping she'd stay, afraid she wouldn't. She looked clean and good and kind, and sometimes said strange and lovely things.

"You are not bad and dirty," she said. "You haven't really killed your heart. It's a fine, red, feeling thing. The crack is the lie."

We talked and talked. Sometimes I wrote down what she said, in a perfect hand, with hearts drawn around the words in red pencil. My foot healed and the pins came out.

And the noise came in, heart-cracking waves of it.

I believed as I had since childhood that the sound would kill me. I tore up the heart-words and threw them in the garbage. I couldn't believe such things. I was crazy! Talking to someone in the mirror? Nonsense! The woman with the real smile stopped saying lovely things to me. Her bright blue eyes turned glassy, then vacant. With my hands over my ears, I swallowed whatever I could find to stop the sound, wherever I could find it.

§

Two more years passed while I picked off bits of me and flicked them around to dangerous strangers as if I were dealing cards. Anything rather than being alone.

Then one night I realized I wanted those pieces back.

I was walking across the road to the store in a long Irish wool cape. I noticed a truck speeding along, trying to make the light. The used-to-be foot, the flip-flopping dragging one attached to the crack inside, stepped purposefully off the curb, welcoming the oblivion of the impact. The other foot, the just-healed one that knew about the blue-eyed woman in the mirror, stepped back onto the curb. I was so close to being struck by the truck that it sucked at my cape in a powerful whoosh and whirled me off my bewildered feet.

I sat on the sidewalk, stunned, acutely aware of what had nearly happened. It seemed I wanted to live, to try again one more time. When I got back to my apartment, I sat down with Georgey clutched in my arms, rocking, rocking, until the mantra of movement eased me to sleep.

Soon after, I met Joe at an AA meeting. His jackhammer sense of humour could break through my darkest moods. He'd seen hard times because of alcoholism, but was now eleven years sober in the AA tradition. He had managed to rebuild his life, and now worked as a stockbroker on Bay Street.

He was a good influence on me, and we became inseparable. We had long, circular discussions about sobriety. I talked about wanting to stop drinking more than anything in the world. He talked about serenity and joy, forgiveness and acceptance—strange concepts that gave me goosebumps. When I took him home to meet my parents, the "look" disappeared from my father's face. I often wondered how long it would take Joe to discover who I really was.

One day when the delirium tremens threatened he took me to the hospital, where I learned about a twenty-eight day treatment offered by the Addiction Research Foundation. Frightened by the allure of the truck's headlights and willing to try again, I committed to the program. I was told that I must stop using substances altogether so that my healing could begin in earnest: no sleeping pills, no alcohol, no pain medication, no amphetamines, no tranquilizers.

I was also told there was an experimental treatment available, a drug called Antabuse that could be inserted under the skin in pellets for those who didn't trust themselves to take it by mouth. It would remain active in the system for six months. Drinking while it was in the system, the doctor said, might cause serious side effects, one of which could be death. Antabuse had proven to be effective in some cases when complemented by psychotherapy and AA meetings. As soon as I completed the rehabilitation program I underwent this procedure, and began to look for work shortly after.

A small firm on Bay Street hired me as a personnel consultant. I loved feeling useful, and worked with care and enthusiasm. At Christmastime I played Santa for the staff party. I put everything I had into that day. I ho-ho-hoed, jiggled my belly as best I could, and listened to each child's gift list with rapt attention.

It made me happy to be part of the firm, and I enjoyed contributing to a common purpose. It seemed that when I believed in something I was dedicated and loyal, honest and hardworking, traits I didn't know I had. I blossomed. I had never worked harder. I was promoted to sales representative and began meeting with personnel managers of major firms.

But the sound was gaining on me. Travelling home on the subway one evening I said to myself, "Shut up. Just shut the hell up." I thought I'd said it in my head until a fellow next to me said menacingly, "You'd better not be talking to me, lady."

Six months later I had the pellet procedure repeated. In the operating room I heard one of the nurses say that vitamin C was used as an antidote for patients who drank while on Antabuse. At a follow-up appointment I overheard someone talking in the waiting room about people they knew of who drank without side effects while using the medication. When I left the doctor's office I bought some vitamin C, took a handful, and went to a restaurant. Only someone insane would do something like this, I thought. I was hopeless, wasting everyone's time, beyond saving.

I ordered a beer, took a sip, and waited; I took another sip, and waited. My face flushed and my hands itched, but nothing else happened. Until the effect of the Antabuse wore off, I continued to drink, with minimal side effects. And the noise faded to a tolerable murmur.

Eventually Joe had to stop seeing me. My drinking was threatening his sobriety, he said. I'd expected it to happen sooner or later, but I missed him terribly, as I did all things good and beautiful that I forfeited to silence the roar. I didn't deserve him, I thought. And that was that.

§

A few weeks later, I was to meet the manager of Canadian Pittsburg Industries for lunch. I believed wholeheartedly that our firm could streamline their hiring practices. That morning I'd worn my new camel suede suit with matching purse and shoes. My hair and makeup were just so. We met in Hy's Restaurant, just around the corner from work. I had a few drinks with him, then stayed on to drink when he left.

As I crossed the street on the way back to work, I fell. A half-full mickey of vodka slid out of my purse and crashed against the curb. Sprawled on the cement, nose scraped and bleeding, nylons torn, I heard the comments of the people gathering around me.

"She's drunk," they said. "Disgusting."

Not a single person offered a hand to help me up.

Burning with shame, I dragged myself back to the office, stopping first at the washroom to fix myself up as well as I could. I looked in the mirror and saw my bloody face, my dishevelled hair, and the streaks in my makeup. I'd break my neck in one of these falls, if the noise didn't kill me first.

She was back in the mirror, the haggard woman with empty eyes.

Then, for a glorious instant, the woman with the real smile and the bright blue eyes appeared. "You deserve to be all you can be," she said.

She vanished.

But I had an idea.

10 · A Geographical Cure

Two weeks later I rested my face against the cool glass of a bus window. Bits of premature spring poked through the icy crust in whiskers of green and brown. Leaning fence posts sported dripping snow hats. Tumbledown barns and stone-pitted meadows whizzed past the window as I pondered my future.

The idea that had come to me after I'd fallen on the pavement, a heap of booze and humiliation, was to move back home to Kingston. Surely being close to my family would help me make some sense of it all. Perhaps I could grow a new heart there, one without an insatiable crack.

I'd made a few trips home before this, and they hadn't all been disasters. I remember one day in particular, one of the happiest of my life, when Dad and I planted a row of cedars at the house on the lake where he and Mom had retired. For a while Dad had seemed to forget what a disappointment I'd been. When he asked for my help, I was deeply honoured. This was land he cherished. We worked as a team, father and daughter, backs bent, our past suspended for a few fragile hours. He dug the hole, then I centred the tree while he filled the cavity with soil. We laughed nervously at nothing in particular, as if we had both sensed there would be little laughter ahead.

As we walked back to the house, I placed one arm around his shoulder and hugged him, pretending this was just another one of many good times we shared. I think he pretended too.

"That was fun, Dad."

"You did a good job. I'm glad you were here to help."

He seemed to like me, at least for the afternoon. I was delighted to be sober and helpful. I hadn't felt such closeness since we played elephant in front of the fireplace years ago. Once again I was the little girl who made him smile, and he was a proud father smiling back with love in his eyes. That night, before the day's memories could become lost in the dark and shrivel into nightmarish distortions, I prayed and prayed to become well for my mountain. I had often prayed such prayers; they hadn't been answered yet, but I was working on it.

The bus pulled into the station and I saw Mom waiting for me. Before she spotted me I feasted on her exquisite face. I'd memorized every line and furrow, and often drew it with my mind when despair loomed. She had always been steadfast and hopeful, even when I must have seemed a wild, fragmented thing, lost to demons she couldn't bear to fathom. More than anything else, I loved her for that.

I put my bags in the trunk and we headed north to Devil Lake. Mom had been supply-teaching that day, and I could tell she was tired.

"I really miss everyone," I said. "Maybe I should move back home."

That was why I'd come today, to ask if she and Dad would mind if I moved back to Kingston.

"Wherever you'd be happiest, honey," Mom replied. I reached over and squeezed her arm. I knew Dad might feel differently.

As we turned into the driveway I saw the cedars Dad and I had planted. Today they looked like sentries ready to repel any attempt to disturb the tranquility of my parents' retirement.

Mom and I climbed up the stone steps, arm in arm. She opened the door and my gaze was drawn across the room to the big window, out over the garden, and clear down to Devil Lake, a panorama I never tired of. Dad was seated with his back to it, an open book in his lap. When he saw me, the look spread across his face as though he'd smelled something rotten.

I sat on the couch in front of the fireplace and for a moment gazed into the fire, hoping to find courage there. As I watched the fire dance, I realized that Dad wouldn't want me to come back. Why would he? My being there would remind him of things he didn't want to think about. He'd told me once that when he looked at me he was reminded of every failure he'd ever had. The question I had rehearsed tiptoed to the tip of my tongue and paused there, warily.

"Would you be comfortable with my moving back to Kingston?" I said, the words tumbling out in a hurry.

"It's up to your mother," Dad said, avoiding my eyes and looking over his shoulder into the kitchen, where Mom was making a salad.

I dragged my disappointment over the carpet and into the kitchen, kissed Mom on the cheek, squeezed her arm, and laid my head on her shoulder, something I'd done a thousand times. "What do you think, Mom?" I said, knowing I could move anywhere I wanted, but fishing for an invitation anyway.

"It would be a good thing for you," Mom said, meaning it. "Maybe once you're settled we could go to a Frank Mills concert at the Grand."

Honoured by her constancy, I was filled with love for that dear woman. Her words deepened my resolve to be well. My ember rose to flaming heights, and I promised myself that I would never, ever take another drink as long as I lived.

Dad was cautious. He'd learned to protect himself against the disappointments. He didn't know about the abuse, all he saw was the acting out. Mom was filled with mother-faith, that bottomless well of hope. After supper she and I made plans, giggling over copious amounts of tea, and circled apartments for rent in the newspaper.

The next day we piled into Mom's beige Chevy and headed for town, mother and daughter with a common mission, a rare and precious time for us. We shared peanuts from a jar she kept under the seat, and every now and then she would pop one out the window, saying, "One for me, one for you, and one for that poor bedraggled crow on the fence post." Mom loved birds.

We rented the first apartment we saw. A small two-bedroom, it was perfect. "One bedroom for an office to study for your degree," Mom said, pride in her voice. It had gleaming hardwood floors, a sprawling kitchen, lots of closet space, and an enclosed backyard for my cat, Georgey. After leaving a deposit, we walked across the street arm in arm to a Simpson-Sears outlet to choose curtains and area rugs from the catalogue. Our hope was so bright that day we surely dazzled everyone we met.

Later, at the lake, Peter and Ann stopped in on their way home from their cottage. Our light-hearted banter and their suggestions for paint and wallpaper were encouraging. Even Dad was affected. At supper, he held up his glass of tomato juice, looked me right in the eye, and sent a blazing father-love smile over our walls and across time. I was breathless with gratitude.

No one knew, least of all me, that addiction, that black-hearted dasher of hope, was making plans as well.

On the way back to Toronto my head filled with ideas. Maybe I could go to university after all. I thought of fixing Mom's hair, a sorely missed ritual. Somehow, some way, I'd make the love stay in my father's eyes. I could do it. I just wouldn't drink anymore. It couldn't be any simpler than that, could it? Being close to my family was what I needed. Spending time with them, showing them I could be strong, would help me stay well.

I didn't know then that being strong was not enough.

I packed and planned, dreamed and hoped, fantasized and made lists. More than anything, I prayed. Praying on my knees was something I hadn't done since I was a little girl. In those far-off days I used to make sure that my out-loud prayers were pure and childlike, so that Mom wouldn't discover the secret. My silent prayers, though, had been about the bad man, about the dark rooms, about eating so much candy my tongue hurt. "Dear God," I'd said in my head, "please make it stop."

Now, decades later, my prayers were much the same. All I wanted was to bring happiness to my family and be loved by them. I was the cause of all our problems, wasn't I? If I just got better, everything would be all right, wouldn't it? I knew I could do it. But the responsibility weighed me down as if I was wearing a suit of lead. "Dear God, please make the cravings stop."

No sooner was I back in Toronto than the fear returned, just as it always did, cocksure and right on time—eager to put me back where I belonged, far down in that fathomless crack. Could I stay sober for my family? What would I say when I was asked about what kind of work I did in Toronto? There were so many gaps in my work history. What would my brother's friends think of me? What would happen if I couldn't keep the light shining in my father's eyes? What if I were to do something to make Mom unhappy? The roar bellowed its lies, and my dreams were sucked into a whirlpool of sound. I was foolish to wish for such fine things. They were not for people like me.

This roar had become more powerful and ruthless than ever before. It gathered intensity, and positioned itself right next to my eagerness for a future with my family. Hope had given it more fuel. My dreams scattered; my decorating lists lay crumpled in the wastebasket.

Going back home was a bad idea. The roar knew it. And I knew it.

So I did what I always did best. I stopped the noise.

Several days after the conversation with my parents, I came to on the kitchen floor. Georgey was licking my face. I tried to get up, but fell down in my own waste. The room began to spin. I felt myself sinking. The ceiling looked bleak and blank, like the canvas of my future. I didn't want to get up, ever. But I realized that my tongue had been badly bitten and would need stitches. Ashamed, I went to the emergency room.

The doctor told me that after having ingested large amounts of alcohol for long periods of time, I must not stop drinking abruptly. Another alcoholic seizure could be fatal. In the future, after a drinking bout, I must take a sedative for a few days, then taper off the medication. He handed me a prescription for a hundred Librium.

I didn't drink a drop as I prepared to move home. I had the pills now, which the doctor said were harmless. Hope was back, my ember re-ignited. I didn't think about the past any more. The roar, that infernal clamour of feelings, simply vanished. I was ready to go home.

§

I'd hired a moving van and the driver was loading the last of my things. I had left my apartment in ruins—not the kind you could see, but the kind that filled the rooms with a death-grey cloud and left the taste of ashes on my tongue. Everywhere there were invisible outlines, like the ones drawn in chalk at a crime scene. As I stood at the door, I could see them: that's where I fell in the bathtub; that's where I fell in the living room; that's where I woke up wondering where four days had gone.

I picked up my purse, pulled the door shut, and walked to the elevator.

All I needed was a new start.

Waiting in the lobby with Georgey in my arms, I felt happier than I had in years. I hugged him close and whispered into his twitching ear, "Mommy won't be sick any more." I swear he understood, for he stopped wiggling and looked up at me. I sucked in a long, hoping breath. "I promise."

§

As we drove along the highway, leaving the city behind, everything seemed as full and ripe as a basket of fruit spilling onto a harvest table. I looked at my watch. It was time for my next pill.

I was brimming with plans for taking courses at the university, making new friends, and showing my family I could make something of myself. Everything would be different now.

Almost there, we drove along the street to my new home. The trees were lush, the sun making shadows of their branches on the school wall across the street from where I would live. The children played in the yard with flailing, endless energy. Memories of my childhood that wasn't slid through my mind and disappeared. Was that an omen? Was it a good one?

The triplex seemed smaller than I remembered. I must paint the door, I thought, as the truck stopped in front of my mother's car. I felt a boulder in my throat when she appeared at the door in her apron. I couldn't get to her fast enough. Mom was from the old school emotionally so she wasn't demonstrative, but her hug would have squeezed the wind out of a polar bear. We clung and cried, not wanting to let go for fear things wouldn't be any different this time.

She'd placed a welcome mat at the front door. A bouquet of gladiolas from her garden stood on the front-window ledge. The countertop in my kitchen was lined with homemade pickles, jam, and canned tomatoes. Freshly laundered and ironed tea towels hung on the cupboard door. Packets of frozen venison in brown paper tied with perfect string bows were stacked in the freezer.

I'll never forget the look on her dear face. Love was there, and a touch of embarrassment too, as though she was self-conscious about showing how glad she was to see me. Her ember was glowing again too.

But my father hadn't come.

It would be two years before the gift arrived, two years of not-so-quiet desperation. I tried. I really did. I was home, close to my family. In the beginning I spent weekends at the lake with my parents. I fussed over Mom, cooked meals, and tidied up. I helped Dad in the garden and tried to make conversation, but it was difficult, like trying to open a tin can with my bare hands.

I got up early and set the table for his breakfast: five prunes in their juice, a pot of tea, toast, margarine, peanut butter, and a small pitcher of milk. I served Mom breakfast in bed, tea and toast with peanut butter cut into little soldiers the way she'd done for me when I was a child, and we'd talk as she ate. She showed me off to the neighbours. Her daughter was home.

It wasn't long before the pills I'd brought from Toronto were gone, and the sadness returned. It drifted in at first as a thin vapour curling around my thoughts, but soon it had become a great looming cloud of dark memories. And from it came the sound. Just one small drink, I promised myself.

Plastic bottles, glass bottles, tall bottles, short bottles, all of them empty, piled up in the trash. I tried to stay sober for weekends at the lake, but it wasn't working. I began to make excuses for not going. I found doctors who were willing to prescribe pills, and dangerous strangers who could ease the loneliness. I slipped further into the crack, one drink at a time.

It had been true all along. I was no good.

I was a liar, a drunk, a junkie, and a whore. And that was that.

The drinking took me to many emergency rooms, brutally unforgiving places back then for an alcoholic woman. The drugs caused wild mood swings. The look was back on my father's face, the confusion and disappointment on Mom's. The look became the sound, and the sound became the roar. My life became a dance with death, and I could not find the strength to stop the music.

A few weeks before the gift came, my father was driving his out-of-her mind daughter to the hospital. He had taken my suicidal references seriously when we'd talked on the phone earlier that day. I had met him at the door with dead eyes, bare feet, and a nightgown stained with blood. The night before, convinced that my family were looking at me from their pictures, which hung on my living room wall, I had smashed the glass in the frames with my fist so that they couldn't see the animal I'd become. I'd quit drinking a few days before and had no pretty pills to stop the hallucinating.

As we drove I kept repeating, over and over, "Blow, Nancy, blow." My ember, so glowing when I first came back home, was nearly out. My seventy-seven-year-old father drove me to my first admission to the psychiatric hospital. I had finally arrived. I was crazy. At least it felt that way to me, and must have looked that way to Dad.

I remember little of the days before or after the ride to the hospital, but I remember my crazed ramblings, and the words of my father: "I would give my life right here and now if I could erase from mankind the memory and knowledge of alcohol."

I was profoundly moved by the innocence behind his words and his heartfelt wish to spare me further pain. He didn't know I was running from the noise. I was just doing what addicts do.

Carefully I wrote down the words my father spoke on that freezing, grey day, and the "blow" words, too, having no idea then what they meant. I spent two weeks in the hospital, but my ember did not resume its glowing.

The gift came because I did what some would call an ugly thing. I did it so that my family would be rid of me. I did it because I felt I had no choice. Hobbled in the nowhere place of addiction, I could no longer bear the memories: the unspeakable things I did in the house across the street, the dragging foot and its humiliations, the nameless, faceless strangers, that look on the faces of those I loved. Eventually the lie born of self-loathing that I saw in my mirror forced me, a frightened child in a desperate woman's body, to act.

I returned home to my apartment leaden with guilt and bearing a plan born in the distorted perception of an addicted mind. I must make sure my mother never cried herself to sleep again, that my father never had to make another trip to the hospital with a crazy woman-child in bare feet in the blood-red dead of winter. I must erase the dark splotch in the mirror that vaguely resembled my face.

I just wanted to stop the sound. I didn't want to die, I just wanted to stop the ugliness of my life from leaking out to infect every dream and promise. I didn't want to die, I just didn't know how to face life.

I walked to the bathroom as sober and drug-free as I am today and peered deeply, longingly in the mirror, hoping to see there the blue-eyed woman who said lovely things. Instead I saw a woman whose face reflected the pain that was poisoning my family and everything I touched.

I must kill her. From a box in the closet I took out an old-fashioned straight razor that had been my dad's. I raised the blade above my head, savagely struck my wrist, and nearly severed my hand. The rubbery artery popped up and pointed accusingly at the mirror. Crimson despair splattered the face that stared out at me.

I walked slowly to my bed—a journey that only a person with a broken spirit could have travelled so calmly. Not wanting to be seen again in a bloody nightgown, I lay down and stretched my arm over the floor. No longer spurting, the blood was now running steadily from the ends of my fingers. I was surprised at how much of it there was.

My indignant ember flickered, fired up, and spoke to me, sharply and insistently. "Get up and call for help," it urged, with more fervency than it had expressed for years. "This is not what you want. This is a lie you've been told by hopelessness. Get up and face your life."

My wise ember knew something I didn't. Pain would be my greatest teacher. I tried to get up but couldn't. My strength was spilling out before my eyes. The shiny-red moving carpet of my life was making its way slowly into the next room, heading purposefully to the front door as if it knew it had an appointment to keep. My eyes closed on my life.

A scream shattered the stillness, then a crash and a yelp. My eyes closed again. When they opened, two paramedics were hovering over me, closing the artery somehow. The pain assured me I was very much alive.

I heard one man speak into a radio. "We are knee-deep in it," he said. "We're just leaving."

I remember thinking how silly they were to exaggerate so, and heard myself laugh. How strange it must have seemed to those men, struggling to save the life of a laughing woman in a purple nightgown while the river of her life headed to the front door.

Later, I learned what happened. The day before, my upstairs neighbour, an untreated manic-depressive, had been having a shouting and banging episode. In an attempt to apologize, she had baked a cake for me and brought it downstairs. When she opened my door she slipped on the blood, which had made it to the exact spot it needed to be to save my life. She screamed when she realized what she had slipped on, and called an ambulance.

I regained consciousness in the hospital atop a gurney, my father's angry, frightened eyes burning down on me. He was a proud man, his daughter was a drunk, and now this. A plastic surgeon had been called in. My arm was wrapped in gauze.

There was an intravenous drip in my right arm, and the gift was flowing into my veins, hidden in the transfused blood. It was disguised as an ugly thing, an almost-taking-of-my-life thing, and it had been given to me by myself.

It would be eighteen years before I knew it had entered my body. It percolated and multiplied there, waiting until the time was right to save me from myself. I would learn to love and cherish its dwelling within me, and I became quite content to have it as a permanent resident.

After the surgery I spent some time on the psychiatric floor. The staff said I shouldn't have lived considering the blood I'd lost. They seemed angry with me for surviving. Apparently hopelessness of that magnitude was unacceptable, even on a psychiatric floor. The messages in their eyes were subtle, but they let me know that I had committed a most grievous sin.

As I lay in bed on the third day, I overheard the head of psychiatry say to the nurse, "She's been here before. Just continue with the Librium. She's a hopeless case."

I will never forget my burning rage. I wrote down this thought: "No one should be considered hopeless until that person alone decides they are." It was a strange reaction for someone who had just performed the ultimate act of hopelessness. I still have the piece of paper to remind me that my ember was always glowing.

After I left the hospital, I began weekly counselling sessions at the Alcohol Referral Centre. In a few months I was working there as a part-time volunteer receptionist. I enjoyed meeting people with a problem similar to mine, and was able to stay sober for months at a time.

A phrase I discovered in the *Big Book* of Alcoholics Anonymous described my dilemma perfectly, and helped to unravel at least one thread of the mystery: "Addiction is cunning, baffling and powerful." That explained the unexplainable, and made sense to me when nothing else in my life did. I made small posters of those words and tacked them up in every room in my apartment, and I carried them, printed on an index card, in my purse.

I began volunteering at Interval House, a place where women and children could safely heal after they'd left an abusive relationship. I could understand why women who felt worthless would repeatedly return to the person who hurt them, and I was saddened at how harshly they were judged. Eventually I was offered a permanent counselling position.

I was stunned when I was nominated for the Kingston Volunteer of the Year Award. To be recognized this way—me, the no-account drunk—was beyond belief. Mom and I walked the few blocks to the award ceremony arm in arm, she wearing her best feather hat and tweed suit even though it was a warm fall night, and I wearing my new taupe linen slacks and ivory cotton blouse. She leaned on me for support, and I was grateful for the chance to press against her.

We climbed the elegant stone steps of City Hall, walked through the foyer and up the magnificent wooden staircase carved over a hundred years before, and found the meeting room. As we sat there, I felt a buzz of excitement in the air and a tingle in the nape of my neck.

When my name was called out, I climbed the stairs to the stage, crossing the fingers of both hands in a last-minute superstitious gesture, fearing Mom would feel let down if I didn't win. Mom had accompanied me to doctors' offices and to hospital emergency rooms, feeling helpless and somehow to blame. This night was for her.

I didn't win the award, but that didn't seem to matter to her. When I looked down from the stage I could see her face glowing, and tears of pride streaming down her cheeks.

§

Only a few short weeks after that glorious night I found myself drinking again. Mom had entrusted me with renting the upstairs rooms in the city house. Apparently it was necessary, for insurance purposes, to have the house occupied. I'd rented one of the rooms to a retired lawyer from Brockville who, as it happened, was an alcoholic. It wasn't long before I was drinking with him, and eventually we became lovers. Soon I was missing work, and I lost the job at Interval House. Then one day the man moved out of the house and disappeared. He didn't tell me he was going, and I never saw him again.

I rarely found myself lonely when I was sober, but as my drinking increased so did my need for companionship. I'd started to attend church services, and one day made friends with a woman who introduced herself as a born-again Christian. But it was her rebellious side I found so strangely appealing. I willingly followed her on her man-hunting escapades to the local bars, and watched her preach there to anyone who would listen. I found it a bit embarrassing, but I could relate to her spiritual confusion, and her company eased my loneliness. I thought I was safe, thought I'd found a true friend. I had no idea I'd put my heart in grave danger, that I was entertaining the enemy.

Our attachment grew and I became enmeshed in her problems. A single mother with several children, she struggled financially and often lacked the basic necessities. I worried about her. Unaware that I was digging myself into a hole of co-dependence, I supplied her with groceries and paid her heating and cable television bills. I loved that woman, trusted her, thought she was my friend. I believed she was who she claimed to be. As she disclosed the details of her life I sensed that my trust might be misguided, but I denied my intuition as my drinking increased and my dependence on her as a trusted confidante grew. I have since learned it is wise to believe people the very first time they show me who they are.

My father shook his fist at me after meeting her. "That woman is trouble," he shouted. "When are you ever going to listen to me?" But I paid no attention. It didn't seem to occur to me that during forty year's experience as a police officer he might have developed a sound instinct about people.

When I was sober and plugged into my instincts I would think, "There is something wrong here." But I didn't trust myself, and our relationship continued. I had no idea that one day I would look back on that time and see her, in my mind's eye, with one hand on her Bible and the other poised above me, ready to rip my heart out.

The following spring, sitting in a bar with some friends, I said to no one in particular, "I feel like dancing."

From close by I heard someone say, "I'll take you dancing."

I turned to see a man, string-bean tall and with thick black hair, standing by the bar, grinning. He wore beige polyester trousers that were a little short, and white ankle socks, their elastic giving way. For some reason I found his lack of concern about his appearance endearing. As we bantered back and forth, I was mesmerized by the sprigs of wiry black hair that poked out from between the bottom of his pants and the tops of his socks. He seemed a little lost and lonely—a kindred spirit, I suppose. We left for a bar up the street that had a dance floor.

We spent that weekend together, and in a few months Dick moved in with me. At the time I was living in and taking care of a six-unit apartment building Dad owned, down the street from the house where I grew up.

Dick had qualities that suited me. He seemed kind, and when things were going his way he had a lively sense of humour. He was emotionally distant, but I hoped that would change. I had no idea he was hiding a great deal. He loved to drink and preferred not to work, although he did drive a cab when he needed money. That suited me fine in the beginning. We meandered through the countryside in his old navy blue Volvo, stopping at quaint bars in picturesque villages and making love in the woods. I fell in love with a fantasy.

Georgey took an instant dislike to Dick. He would glare down from his various perches like a hairy gargoyle, and sometimes he would hiss and arch his back in unabashed feline disapproval.

Our apartment was small and dark, and although I was used to living in dim caves, Dick couldn't stand to be inside. I bought an antique wooden cruiser, and Dick was content to spend most days working on the boat at the marina and drinking. I stayed at home and drank. On weekends we cruised through the Thousand Islands. The sun and fresh air were healing, and I gradually began to feel safe. But underneath the surface of the fantasy an unwelcome notion squirmed like a discontented worm: good things never last.

Georgey, now sixteen years old, had been a staunch friend and an excellent judge of character, and caring for him had helped me develop a tender sense of responsibility. It appeared that I was his keeper, although on a deeper level I knew that he was mine. He'd spoon against my belly on the long, long nights, nestling against the dark-rumbling gut of my choices, comforting me in the lost times, a guard against my frequent musings about suicide.

Tests revealed that he had developed congestive heart failure. It was time, the veterinarian said. I stayed with Georgey as he was laid on his side and the needle slid into his leg. He looked up at me, trusting that I knew what was best. His eyes closed. Through a storm of tears, grief-hard choking sounds, I begged his forgiveness.

It seemed fitting to bury him under a giant purple iris in the backyard. He'd often hidden behind the green fanning spikes, alert, stalking-still, his eyes glistening amber in the sunlight. Then he'd pounce on an unsuspecting butterfly or an unwary mouse. Occasionally I'd find a dead bird beside the bed. I chose to think it was a special gift, and never scolded him for it.

I nailed two pieces of wood together in the shape of a cross and wrote on it in waterproof magic marker, "Here lies my friend."

A few days later, the veterinarian's office called. A three-year-old cat named Goochie had been left, with a touching letter requesting that he be placed in a suitable home. Apparently his favourite people-food was Kraft Dinner, chicken, and scrambled eggs, preferably topped with a little Parmesan cheese. That I adored Parmesan cheese on my eggs too was no doubt a sign: Goochie was to come home with me.

He was a storm of activity. A pure white shorthaired Persian with eyes blue as a summer sky, he claimed the apartment as his personal gym. He tested the weight of drapes for climbing potential and knocked the Kleenex box off the refrigerator to clear a stalking perch. He seemed to think of himself as a dog, for he made his needs known in a cross between a yip and a growl. He let me know he was there to stay.

In 1987 I joined a women's recovery group and managed to stay sober for two years (although I still needed prescribed sedatives and anti-depressants). Dick and I were married a year later at City Hall. Our honeymoon was a trip to Ottawa through the Rideau Canal system. We watched the baby ducks cavort in the water, delighted in the sunsets, and cooked on an old propane range in the galley. I thought life couldn't get any better. We stopped in Westport to take Mom for a spin. She was glowing that day, delighted that I'd finally settled down.

I thought I was content, but as my sobriety continued I discovered something disturbing: my feelings for Dick didn't match the fantasy.

But anything was better than being alone.

The summer Dick and I were married I received a call from Ruthie, whom I hadn't seen or talked to for twenty years. She said that she'd begun to remember some of the abuse she had suffered from her father, and asked if he had hurt me too. I was shocked that she remembered so little, but I understood how agonizing remembering can be, and that the mind, while it can be an efficient protector, can also be a powerful enemy. Apparently an investigation had begun, but had then petered out. Now someone wanted to do a television documentary on the case, which had gained some notoriety, and they needed someone to corroborate Ruthie's account.

After our conversation, Ruthie was convinced I'd remembered accurately, that my memories weren't "maybe" or "sort of" memories. She was right. It was as if his handprints had been branded on my soul. She asked if I'd be willing to be interviewed. Wanting to consider my parents' feelings before I agreed, I decided it was time to tell them.

Of course my parents didn't know that their former neighbour was a pedophile. They didn't know about the dark rooms in the house across the street, about the insanity that lingered in the halls. They didn't know about the other bad men who lived there, or about the card games. They couldn't possibly have known that every time a player won a hand, he would be offered my body as a human prize.

Dick and I were sitting on lawn chairs at the cottage with Mom, Dad, Peter, Ann, and the kids when I shared with my parents everything that Ruthie told me. Then I told them that for six-and-a-half years her father had sexually abused me. I explained that if I were to come forward it might help other victims.

When I finished, my father jerked around to face me, his upper lip curled in disgust like the pinky-smooth edge of a conch shell.

"You probably asked for it," he hissed.

All the red handprints on my young body, all the blows I'd inflicted upon myself, and all the hurts I'd collected in my life could not compare with the impact of those words.

My memory took a snapshot of that day. I wish it hadn't. The air died and the world stood still. The leaves stopped rustling on the branches. The golden brush strokes of the sun faded from the lawn. Words that wished they had never been uttered hung in the cacophonous stillness.

I pretended I wasn't shattered. My father pretended I didn't exist. And Mom went to her denial place, a kinder, safer place, because the conflicts between those she loved hurt too much.

I began to hate Dad. The feeling sat inside me, a sour pain, curdling my love for him. How could I hate my own father, my mountain? It swirled round and round, spinning me out of myself into a cloud of confusion. I couldn't fathom or escape the love-hate, love-hate, love-hate.

It was clear that we were not to talk of this ugly thing. Dad's words hung in the air, suspending love and forgiveness in a time capsule. It would be fourteen years before they could be put away in a special box for mended things. They would have their day.

In the meantime, I made a thousand excuses for his words. There was not a day I did not remember them. I understand what would have gone through a father's mind in the few seconds between my account and his response, the terrible guilt he must have felt for not having been able to protect me when I was a child. The pain delivered by my revelation must have been so great that he did what I've done a thousand times: he lashed out at the messenger.

It was the thundering silence that followed that did the real damage. A quiet storm raged between us. We flailed at one another, drowning in word wounds and gasping for the breath that would only come with forgiveness.

§

The following winter Dick and I flew to Jamaica with friends. While we were there my mother had a stroke. One month before I would have celebrated two years of sobriety, I began to drink again.

13 · Mother Love, Death, and Betrayal

An angel was watching. He was ready to swoop down, knowing, as angels do, the precise moment when the cracks in the wall I'd forged against the world would split apart. And out I'd fall, tumbling, tumbling.

Soon. Very soon.

For now, I had a purpose. Mom needed me. Her right side was paralyzed, and she was in a nursing home. She never complained, but I know she was downhearted and frightened. I promised her I'd be there for her always, and I was, until the day she died.

I was thankful my favourite season had arrived. Fall always had a way of turning my senses up a notch. Today it smelled tart and crisp as an Ida Red apple, and it helped blur the edges of the sadness I felt for Mom. The air was so clear that from the corner I could see clear across the St. Lawrence to the Wolfe Island ferry dock. I had just cut the grass, and the earthy smell curled up from the backyard, licking the air.

I had decided to begin work on my degree, and was excited to have something to look forward to. My disease had taken its toll, so I wasn't able to work full-time. I suspected Dick was cheating on me, but chose not to make it real by confronting him. It felt as if there wasn't much air left in my lungs to fan my ember, but I hoped that going back to school would fill them again.

I enrolled at Queen's University in Pharmacology 101. The classes, the young people, and the sense of purpose were exhilarating. Mom was excited about my going back to school; she enjoyed having me study at the nursing home while she slept. Occasionally she'd open her eyes for a moment or two and a smile of pride would appear. Too few of them had touched her lovely face where I was concerned.

I achieved an 83-percent average on the course. Surprised, and afraid that no one would believe me, I asked Professor

Racz to write a letter stating the specifics of the course, the date, and my grade. At the nursing home, I showed Mom a copy of the letter. She smiled and said what she always did: "I knew you could do it, honey." I often wondered what it was she saw that so thoroughly escaped my own knowing. She must have had a special gift, a mother's way of seeing beyond behaviour into the heart of her young. I was told that as soon as I left she beetled down the hallway and stopped anyone she met to show them the letter. She started referring to "my Nancy" this and "my Nancy" that when she talked to the staff. I was delighted to know I'd made Mom happy.

She kept the letter in a bag slung over the back of her wheelchair until she died. And for years afterward I carried it in my purse. Even now I sometimes read that yellowed piece of paper, tattered and worn from repeated openings. Each time, I'm reminded that there was always air in my lungs. I just didn't know it.

I hated the nursing home, hated that Mom had to be there. Its dreary corridors wound around rooms that smelled of sterility. Worried that the smell only camouflaged bacterial secrets, I never trusted it. As I passed those rooms and the elderly, cast-off human beings who lived in them, I knew that they knew they were biding their time. I resented that place, because it transformed people—parents, sisters, friends—into resigned silhouettes with necks that strained toward the door, looking for visitors who never came.

Even in that awful place those six years were a special time for Mom and me. We acted silly, laughing and laughing as if we were making up for all the tears that had been shed. I painted each of her toenails a different colour, and I taught her how to swear. We'd have practice sessions, and the cursing seemed to give her some measure of control, a way to vent the frustrations of her not-so-wonderful life. She'd giggle like a naughty schoolgirl after a particularly feisty cursing session, then fall asleep with a smile at the corners of her mouth. I watched her as she slept, saddened that she had lost her grand height, that she was so small in the hospital bed.

That was a mending time for us. For several years I visited most days, and kept my drinking down to a nip in the washroom to hold the shakes at bay until I got home. Mom pretended she couldn't smell the liquor; I pretended she didn't smell it. Her denial of the shredded state of my life was just a mother's selective way of seeing things, an effort to protect her love for me. That love was nestled in the core of her, in her mother-heart, ancient and powerful. That time for us was my gift to her. I became the mother. I was a good mother. It is one of the few things in my life that I'm proud of.

In order to visit Mom more frequently, Dad had moved from his home in the country into the city house, where I grew up. It sat across the street from the house with the dark rooms, and half a block down from the apartment building where I lived. We were all pressed together in one block, young and old, past and present, keeping our secrets and pretending.

I tended to Dad's needs, waiting to catch a crumb of approval. He didn't like me very much. I kept remembering his words: "You remind me of every failure I've ever had." As a man who had reached ninety-two years of age, he must have felt he'd earned the right to be outspoken and direct. But I've learned that honesty without compassion is punishment, plain and simple.

§

If only Dad and I could have talked things through. Instead, we did our stick walk, marching left-right, left-right, in rigid denial, so afraid that if words were spoken the pain would become real. I continued to try to find a way to stop the dreadful parade, to make him really see me. Now I can understand what we were doing. I needed his approval so desperately that I was willing to become a fraud. I pretended to be who I thought he wanted me to be. He pretended that he didn't know exactly what I was up to. Eventually our true selves dwindled away until only our shadows remained.

Dad was failing rapidly, and he soon joined Mom in the nursing home. It was hell for him. To watch a powerful man losing control of all that he valued—mobility, strength, and

independence—was difficult. The verbal and emotional abuse
he directed at me was staggering. He told me he didn't love
me, and hadn't for twenty years.

A few months before he died, Mom offered to pay for shoes
I'd recently purchased. I'd had an orthotic made, and it would-
n't fit into my other shoes. Mom kept a cheque book in her
drawer at the nursing home and would give small amounts to
family members on special occasions. She had to use her non-
dominant hand because of the paralysis, and would flop her
weak hand over the paper to steady it. Her signature was
barely legible, but it was hers, she said, and made her feel she
was capable of doing something on her own. She put everything she had into making her signature as neat as possible,
with a slight smile of independence playing at the corners of
her mouth.

The next time I came to visit, she was crying. She said Dad
had forbidden her to write a cheque for the shoes, and threatened to take away her cheque book. I stomped up the hall into
his private room and stood before his bed, knees trembling.
"How dare you be so cruel! How dare you! I don't care about
the shoes, but that cheque book meant the world to Mom!"

The strangest thing happened. He began to flail his arms,
carving jagged circles in the air, pushing words, hissed whis-
pers, into the air. "I'm at peace. I'm at peace. I'm at peace," he
mumbled.

I knew about frantic mantras blurted to no one in particular. I'd used them to contain my fragmented sanity by the
sheer force of repetition. But his disoriented mantra frightened me. I backed out of the room, afraid to turn my back to
him, afraid I'd harmed him and he might need me. As I did,
an idea formed. I swung around so sharply that I almost fell,
and hurried out the door on a mission to reduce the distance
between us.

At a drugstore I picked out a blank card. Shaking, weak
with fear (for I rarely stood up to him), but intent on sharing
a meagre bit of my own hard-won experience, I wrote these
words for my father, my mountain: "Peace cannot live in a

heart devoid of forgiveness." When I got back to the nursing home he was asleep. I lay the card on his lap, gently, as if it was my beating heart I offered.

The phone was ringing as I entered my apartment. When I answered, there were no words, just an old man's sobbing. He said nothing for a while, the silence as expansive as the wall between us. It was resonant with a humility that could not become sound.

"It's okay Dad. It's okay," I said, as if he were a child who needed soothing. I let him cry, savouring the sounds, honoured to be privy to such a well-concealed part of a man I loved so desperately. All the unspoken love, the misdirected disappointment, all rolled into one word over and over, never becoming the completed sentence that would have healed us. "I'm, I'm, I'm" — then tears, as if that one word had taken decades to form. "I'm, I'm ..." he stammered.

I knew that he couldn't say the words, that he didn't know how. It was not his way. The bitter disapproval was too old, too embedded in his very own heart-crack. Wordlessness had kept our wounds open and raw. But he knew he had tried to say he was sorry, not for the cheque book but for a lifetime of regret, and I knew it too.

Things changed between us after that. Not in words or actions, but in the air between us, which became less electric with grudge and blame. A few months later he began to talk to me, revealing fragments of himself. The more he shared, the easier it seemed to be for him. As he spoke I was shocked to discover that there were sorrows in my father's life that did not involve me, that I was not responsible for all his unhappiness. I had tortured myself with guilt for decades because I thought I was.

One day he told me something that touched me deeply, something that explained a great deal to me. As a boy he had suffered unrelenting poverty, and had watched his parents work themselves to death. Through force of will he had risen out of poverty to become a respected member of the police force. But it seems that that had not been enough for him. He said that when he was thirty-nine years old and recovering from a near-fatal bout with typhoid fever in the Ongwanada Hospital in Kingston, he'd made a vow. If he survived, he would become "a somebody."

"But somewhere along my journey," he said, "I lost my very self. What good is my money now? Your mother's in a nursing home. I'm going blind."

I respected the endeavours that had enabled a poorly educated man to achieve success. Growing up, I'd developed a love-hate relationship with money. I have often wondered if in the back of my mind I hadn't blamed him for being too busy renovating houses to protect me from the bad man. But he gave me a glimpse into his heart that day, and I finally understood that we weren't so different after all.

A few days later, as I was sitting beside his bed, reading to him, he crooked his finger for me to come closer. "Bring me sleeping pills," he whispered.

"What for?" I asked, knowing perfectly well what he intended.

"You know."

"I won't," I said. " I couldn't." I was sorry for his despair, but confused, and angry too. I felt that on some level his request was a test. Did I love him enough to help him end his life? Did I love him enough not to?

Just before he died, he told me that he could never live up to my expectations. I was shocked. I had blamed him my whole life for disapproving of me because I didn't live up to his. I understand us now. It is as clear as the water of Dad's beloved Devil Lake that I'd constructed my own sorrow. I'd made him a mountain when maybe he just wanted to be an ordinary hill. I'd placed him so high on a pedestal that he couldn't see me, and I couldn't touch him.

When I discovered he was just an ordinary man, I felt betrayed, as if he had tricked me into believing he was something he wasn't. And he resented me for making him strive for the unattainable, for making him appear a failure. How sad is the dance that families do, that frantic jig of expectation and blame. Words would have stopped the music. If only.

I knew he had to shut me out emotionally as a defence against his pain. It must have grieved him to watch his daughter damage herself. I understand the dynamics of it now. One by one, my family and friends built walls around their hearts. It was their way of coping with the smashing of a human life right before their eyes. I'm grateful now they had that defence against their pain. My defences were alcohol, pills, food, and anything else that would numb me.

When he developed congestive heart failure, Dad was moved from the nursing home to the hospital. At the end, he slept or was unconscious for days. Every day, I sat with him, talking softly while he was somewhere else in his mind or out of it, between life and death. As I watched him sleep, breathing his raggedy, shallow breaths, I willed him to love me. I wondered whether he was really asleep, or just pretending. Did he keep his eyes closed so that he wouldn't see me at the end of his life, a blatant failure, staring him in the face?

Worried we wouldn't have time, I pulled words, mumbled sentences, choking, ragged pleas for forgiveness, up out of the decades of guilt, and spilled them into the sterile air. Sputtering a lifetime of sadness and fear, I tried to explain everything, hoping he could hear, terrified he'd wake up and wishing he would. My frantic pleas for forgiveness swirled around that awful green room while death stood at the door. Grateful to be freed, those words leapt from my heart with all the pain a daughter can feel when she knows her father is ashamed of her. Those flying words connected with his dying heart. No one can convince me otherwise.

He died at the end of that week. The anger I felt for his leaving before I had a chance to make him love me again was full and ripe, infecting anyone near. I was relieved he was gone, but I wanted him back too. My mind whirled like a dog trying to catch its tail.

§

The thoughts of spring failed to lift my sense of impending loss. My mother was failing rapidly. I felt as if I was slowly sinking into a stagnant pool. I realized that Dick and I had been two needy people looking for someone else to help us make our dreams come true, pressing against each other once in a while, thinking passion could make it all right, hoping the other wouldn't notice that the caring had stopped.

I'd lost respect for Dick long before. But I hated change, as many addicts do, even if the price for remaining in an ailing union was mental, emotional, and spiritual decay. So I clung to the relationship like a mother bear who can't give up her dead cub even after it has decomposed and filled her den with its stench.

I suppose that before the details of my father's will were disclosed, the notion that I would likely inherit a large sum of money had a certain appeal for Dick. But my father, in his wisdom, had left my share of the inheritance, the six-unit apartment building I was living in, in trust. I wasn't as attractive once it turned out that my long-awaited inheritance was under lock and key. After the will was read, Dick became sloppy in his adulterous deceptions, and I had to face what I'd long suspected.

The marriage ended in May 1994. I blamed Dick for not being my knight in shining armour. He blamed me for not fulfilling his dreams. How strange we humans are! We expect others to fill us up, and when the emptiness remains, we hate.

When he came back to pick up his things, he said, "I don't love you. I never loved you. It was all about the money. That's the most honest I've ever been with you."

I suppose his honesty was commendable. Those words, however, did what he'd intended: they nearly killed me. He had found someone else to blame for his failures, and I sank into a sea of rum. It took me four painful years to realize that when he left me he'd handed me the world.

A few weeks after he left, the phone rang. I'd been sober for three weeks, and the roar was working on me. I was alone in the apartment, except for Goochie. I was waiting, pushing invisible bits of nothing around the kitchen table. I had been expecting the call, but I wasn't prepared for what I heard:

confirmation that my trusted friend, the born-again Christian, was the other woman. I clearly recall how calm and analytical my initial response to that devastating news was. I supposed that, given the right circumstances, anyone might be capable of adultery. But I couldn't help feeling that there must be some unwritten moral code between women friends that would prohibit this kind of betrayal.

Then the terrible truth sliced through my mind. I knew that she desperately wanted a man in her life. I'd heard that she had taken her preaching from the bars into the Kingston Penitentiary to look for a suitable candidate, and when she found one she had married him. When that failed, she had turned to another easy target, her best friend's husband.

When the call came I'd been standing beside the counter that stretched six feet along the kitchen wall. I felt myself slump against it for support. The words pressed me to my knees, and I let myself give in to gravity. I lay my head on the linoleum, a few inches from Goochie's box. Under the fridge the bits of food that had escaped the broom looked like a mirage of distant mountains. The pungent odour of the litter box forced me back into reality. I didn't want reality, though. I wanted a drink.

I lifted myself up, and felt as though I'd snap in two if I didn't break something. I pulled a hammer out of the kitchen drawer and looked around for something to destroy. I slammed it onto the glass tabletop, and then went on smashing, smashing the wooden frame, even after the glass top had caved in on itself. Chunks of glass flew across the room, ricocheted off the walls and cupboards, and landed on the floor.

I walked over the broken glass and pulled a chair in front of the entryway so that Goochie wouldn't cut his paws. The jagged shards cut into my feet, but that meant nothing compared to the wound in my chest. I made my way to the bed, tracking a ten-year marriage and a twelve-year friendship in red.

Clutching my stuffed Rusty dog to my chest, I rolled from side to side, side to side, hoping the movement would stop the ripples of pain. The room tilted, my stomach heaved, and whimpering sounds came from my mouth. I didn't realize how loud my anguish was until I heard a knock on the door.

"Nancy?" It was the medical student who lived in the next apartment. "Nancy, its Bill. Open up."

The bed was quicksand and my heart was leaden. I couldn't extract myself. But the knocking, then the pounding, then the frantic rattling of the door frame gave me strength.

"I'll bust the door down if I have to," he shouted. "I just need to see you're okay."

The mattress finally gave me up, and I stumbled to the kitchen and opened the door. Bill stood in the doorway, his eyes big as oranges. I must have been a frightening sight against the gruesome backdrop, a cloth dog pressed against my face, little puddles of blood forming around my feet.

"Jesus, Nancy, it sounded like someone was being murdered in here! What in God's name happened to your feet?" He stepped inside, his eyes wary, taking in the broken glass, the hammer, and the blood. He led me by the arm into the living room and sat me down on the couch.

"Don't move. I'll be right back." I heard my apartment door shut, then open again a few minutes later. He'd returned with a first aid kit, and he tended to my cuts. His eyes were grave, his hands calm and gentle. He used tweezers to remove the shards of glass, and wrapped my feet in gauze.

His kindness meant the world to me, and I told him everything.

The pain of having been betrayed lingered, but focusing on Mom helped. Before her stroke she'd loved to drive—one of my nicknames for her was "Hotrod Carm." As a supply teacher well into her seventies, she had burned up the country roads on the way to class, dust trails billowing behind the car. Sometimes the odd peanut (her after-school snack) or a hat or a scarf would fly out the window.

After her stroke, she often remarked how much she missed driving her old car, a beige 1982 Chevy Biscayne, and each time she did I'd notice the same regret misting her dear old eyes. Her situation was a continual cause of sadness for me, and I wanted to do something to bring a little joy into her life. My plan was to secretly earn my driver's licence, and then surprise her by driving her car when I picked her up at the nursing home. I'd be able to extricate her on weekends from the tangle of resigned, shapeless forms that shuffled along the halls, and I'd have a chance to fuss over her. I couldn't wait to see the look on her face.

After Dick left, Mom suggested that I move into the house where I grew up. The handsome two-storey red brick that Mom purchased in 1939 was a hundred years old and in poor repair. I started to renovate, with Mom's escape scenario in mind.

I painted the kitchen walls white and the trim in forest green, her favourite colour, which matched the ceramic tiles exactly. A space containing a water heater was converted into a handsome wheelchair-accessible bathroom, and I made inquiries into having a ramp built at the front door. She could come every weekend if she wanted.

My driving lessons carried on. Mom's Chevy was a rusted-out old barn of a thing. One day when a friend and I were having an informal lesson, the brakes that had just been checked didn't respond, and the car hurtled down the street, whizzing through stop signs and red lights. I headed for an open laneway so that I wouldn't hit anyone. Although it took the bark off an old maple tree before shuddering to a steaming stop, the car came through with hardly a scratch, and so did I. I hoped it would hold up for Mom's surprise.

Each time I mentioned to Dad my idea of learning to drive, it had resulted in such a commotion of arm-waving that I dropped the subject. I couldn't blame him, considering my drinking history, but the result was that at every driving lesson my memory reluctantly slid back over the last two decades of our relationship. After he died, I began to do things he'd previously disapproved of. He'd scoffed at the suggestion that I might put a flower garden in the backyard of the apartment building. "A waste of money," he said. "You'll never be able to take care of it." The spring after he passed away, I dug several beds and planted impatiens, petunia, white coneflower, portulaca, sweet william, phlox, pansies, nasturtiums. I pressed the earth carefully around each seedling, and watered diligently, weeded with a vengeance.

I redecorated my apartment—another "waste of money"— nothing extravagant, just touches of colour here and there to exercise my independence muscle. Feeling rebellious, I began to talk to Dad, muttering silly things like "Girls need to do girl things" and "Every woman worth her salt would have a flower garden" while I hung cheerful yellow-and-blue striped curtains in the kitchen, knowing full well that my rebellion was as hollow as he was dead.

On the kitchen cupboards I stencilled flowerpots with sassy abstract flowers, each petal a different colour, and lay a dusty rose carpet in the living room over drab grey tiles that Dad had installed forty years earlier. As the carpet went down, I muttered, "There, don't you see? That's much better." I ordered burgundy and pink cushions and curtains. Dad hated pink. "A frivolous color, no substance at all," he'd say. I painted the bedroom a soothing ivory cream with a beige and lemon-yellow flowered border, and casually scattered *ten* new cushions (Dad would have a fit, for surely one, or none at all, would have been more sensible) with golden braid and tassels on the bed. I felt a hand reach out from the grave to squeeze the pleasure out of each task. Death doesn't end anything.

All my life Dad objected to what I said and didn't say, wore or didn't wear, did or didn't do. If I mentioned planning to do something, he'd bore a hole in my enthusiasm with a scathing look and say, "For God's sake, Nancy, what's wrong with your head?"

Seeking his approval till the very end, I begged for crumbs —a half-smile, or a day without his reminding me of my failures. But I couldn't stand up to him; I continued to be a slick imposter, only a sliver of my real self.

I listened intently one day as he described an irritating eye condition he had. His eye was itchy-sore, and it interfered with his reading, one of the few things that gave him pleasure. His eyesight had been failing, and I knew he was worried about impending blindness.

Eager for a snippet of father-daughter intimacy, I mentioned that mites lived in our eyelashes and eyebrows. "Maybe that could be the problem," I said. "We could go to the doctor together to see if there was a prescription that would help."

He jerked his head around to face me and said, as if he was trying to spit out something that tasted foul, "Where'd you learn about mites, in the *National Enquirer*? What nonsense!"

When I told him I was thinking of taking a course at the university, he said, "You might as well flush the tuition money down the toilet. You never finish anything."

But usually his put-downs were more cloaked. It would be as if I'd been cut but didn't know exactly where. Maybe I would use his displeasure as an excuse for avoiding the pain of more failures. Whatever the reason, I went back for more and more, hoping it could be different between us.

I had no idea then that it was himself he loathed.

§

In September of 1994, the bad man came back into my life. Ruthie called to say she was remembering more. She remembered the old house—the upper rooms that were rented to older single men, and the black-hearted sickness that stole through the dark hallways. She remembered enough to know that she and I had been tossed back and forth like pieces of meat. I'd always believed that her memory had been shut down to save her sanity, but the pain was still there, festering inside, a bubbling brew of heart poison. In order to keep it there she had been swallowing, and now weighed well over three hundred pounds. I cannot see an obese person now and not wonder.

One day she came for a visit, and we decided that it might help her memories along if she were to see the inside of the house. We walked across the street and knocked on the door. When a man answered, we told him that Ruthie was trying to remember more of her childhood and that seeing inside might help. He agreed to show us around.

We walked through the pretty stained-glass doors. A claw from the past raked across my genitals, then nothing. Ruthie's memories weren't triggered at all. It was strange that we weren't more affected by just being there. But we were good little soldiers. We understood how well the armour we wore was able to deflect the pain. I'd been drinking that week, so was temporarily reprieved from feeling, and Ruthie's defences against her pain were as powerful as they had ever been.

New evidence had surfaced and the case had been reopened. The bad man was eighty-three years old now, and according to several recent victims' statements he was still playing grisly games with little people, defiling their bodies, mangling their futures. Maybe justice would prevail against this cowardly monster whose atrocities were committed upon defenceless children in the dark. After a gruelling interview by the Crown attorney it was determined that I would be a reliable "historical witness."

For months there were questions, meetings with the Crown attorney, and preparations for the trial. A kind, soft-spoken detective came to take my statement. My fear of not being believed grew like a fungus. All the shadowy, hovering images of the dark rooms returned. When I slept, I dreamed of it.

When I awoke, I walked with it. Painful scraping fingernails, the smell of sour smothering flesh, the hissed threats against my family, and the never-ending pounding fear that I would somehow cause them harm. Those images stalked me, shrouded me in head-hanging shame until I thought I would die from the memory of it.

I didn't think anyone would believe that men played endless games of cards in those dark rooms, hunched over their hands, drooling at the thought of a ripe juicy prize. How could anyone believe they were playing not for money, but for little human beings? I explained my fear to the detective. He said, in the kindest voice I'd ever heard, "I've spoken to other victims in this case, and card games are a common denominator in their stories."

Touched by his compassion, I felt validated, knowing he wasn't obliged to share that information. Having worked on similar cases, he knew that victims grow up with a staggering fear of not being believed. He didn't minimize the seriousness of my experiences. He didn't once subtly suggest that maybe I was mistaken, or that I should just put it behind me. I knew what happened when I tried to put things behind me before first putting them in front. They hunted me down like prey.

When I searched his face for contempt or judgment, he met my eyes. He'd read between the lines in my victim impact statement. He'd seen the look in my eyes before.

But the feeling-noise thundered. All the defences that I'd collected since I was five years old—the food, the alcohol, the drugs, the relationships, the shopping—were failing me, their power to muffle was diminishing. They had turned on me and had now themselves become the problem. I couldn't see that anything would ever change. I began collecting pills. I would dump unused prescriptions into a bag, and each month I would add some of my current medications to the stockpile.

But for now, Mom needed me.

The bad man finally pleaded guilty, so there was no need for a trial. Dozens of victims attended his sentencing, all of them wearing his brand, but I wasn't among them. My victim impact statement was the one the Crown attorney picked to read, but I was still afraid of him, and couldn't attend his sentencing. I was still afraid, still a child. And he was still the bad man.

He was sentenced to three years in Kingston Penitentiary. I suppose that might work out to one child per week of incarceration. His accommodations were just down the hall from Clifford Olsen's, but unlike Olsen he hadn't killed his victims outright. He had used his dirty fingers to gouge out gaping holes in our self-esteem, and his stinking bulk to smother our futures.

I wasn't validated by his sentence, but I didn't blame him for the squandering of my life, either. I had plowed my own fields. What he did do, painfully well, was taint the seed.

After that, Ruthie and I kept in touch for a while, but geography prevented a closer friendship. She'd grown into a lovely woman with a fine family, but her eyes and body told her story well. Instead of alcohol and drugs, she had used food to deal with her demons.

§

My mother's death the following May was a door slamming shut, cutting off the only light left in my life. She died peacefully in her sleep, free at last of a shrivelling body, an ocean of regret, and a broken heart.

I can understand now that the recent events in my life—the betrayal by my girlfriend and my husband, Dad's death, the court case, and Mom's death—were just life doing what life did. But at that time I wasn't prepared. Preparedness comes with learning to cope along the way. I had not learned. I could not cope.

At the nursing home, I stretched across my mother's chest and wrapped my arms around her as tightly as I could. I clung to her, afraid to loosen my grip for fear a gorge would open up and swallow me. That night I felt something in me die too, at least in the part of me that was still living. That shred of hope she had kept alive in me vanished the minute her sweet, generous heart stopped beating. The only one who loved me no matter what was gone.

When her casket was lowered into the ground, I vowed never, ever to take another drink as long as I drew breath. That was the only thing she wanted for me.

But, still a middle-aged child, I hadn't learned any grief-soothing ways other than numbing myself with alcohol, drugs, and food. The losses that touch every life were too much for me. For months after Mom's death, I'd chatter to her incessantly, groping for topics, certain that silence would slay me. I didn't know how to miss her. So I did what I did best. At least I knew how to do that.

Each month, more pills were dropped into the bag.

Soon, very soon.

The driving lessons came to a dead halt: I skidded into the beginning of the almost-end. Having promised Mom I'd do right by our family home, I continued to renovate the house that Mom had left me, the house where I grew up. I changed the four front rooms on the second floor into rental units for graduate students to supplement my income. It made me feel good to have something to do. I had a little brick cottage on the house property renovated, to be rented the following September. There was also some income from the apartment building Dad had bequeathed to me.

Over the years, I had shared with countless therapists my strange notion that I could get well only after my parents died. It had felt odd each time I mentioned it. I had no idea at the time what it meant, but I sensed it powerfully. Maybe I thought that when my parents were gone their presence would no longer remind me of the pain I'd caused them, and I would be able to free myself of that pain too.

My divorce was proceeding. The greed in the settlement request, considering the circumstances that ended our marriage, shocked me. You think you know someone, then their truth nearly kills you.

I dreaded the Thanksgiving and Easter holidays that had gathered the family together when Mom was alive. I was alone. Self-inflicted pain is still pain.

I slept during the day. The nights, when no one could see, became my wandering times. I travelled through my house like a ghost looking for its severed head. Flipping frantically through family albums, I tried to find a reason to be. There was nothing to show me who I was, where I belonged. The face in the mirror when I dared to look seemed disfigured since Mom left. Sometimes I caught a glimpse of a gaping hole where my well-practised smile used to be. It was getting harder and harder to pretend.

The depression frightened me. It was one thing to have a bag of death that grew fatter every month, a bag I chose to fill, a bag that was for me to decide when and where to use it. It was quite another to feel a darkness drawing over me without my permission, promising suffering such as I'd never known. When I shared that with the doctor, he checked me into Scott's Clinic— for a rest, he said. I rested all right. I slept for two weeks, stumbling to the table for meals, or to the washroom, and left in a daze with three bottles of pills: 100 fifty-milligram Librium, 100 Halcyon, 100 Prozac—three hundred ways to avoid facing life.

The fire started around noon one day in September. I had been sleeping around the clock, and I awoke to the sound of crashing glass. A man in a yellow suit was breaking my bedroom window. The heat surrounded us, the smoke cut into my throat. My mattress was smouldering. I was dragged from the bed dazed and numb. Three separate fires were burning on the carpet in the connecting room, small bonfires ready to explode. Next to my bed a chair piled high with clothes was ablaze. Curtains hanging near the chair were on fire; pointed orange teeth were taking greedy bites.

The water convulsed its way through the hose up the stairs, down the hall, and splashed into the bedroom. The mattress was thrown outside my front door for all to see.

To this day I don't know who raised the alarm. Someone else, something else was blowing on my ember.

It was not my time.

Soon after, I contacted the fireman who had been at the scene, hoping he could tell me who had called the fire department. He wasn't able to supply that information, but he said he'd never seen anything so odd. My bed had been completely burned except for the corner where I'd been curled in a fetal position sucking my thumb. My white cotton nightgown had several burn holes, but there was not a mark on my body except for a tiny red blister on my neck where a spark had landed.

My body had been saturated with alcohol, topped up with pills, and I'd been smoking. I was living alone in the house then and would have been quite happy to have burned to death. To have been rescued infuriated me.

I moved the mattress to the backyard and covered it with a tarp. The stuffing was gone, burned to nothing, and the metal springs were melted and twisty. But the upper right-hand corner, where I was sleeping, was untouched. From time to time I would lift the tarp to peer in wonder at the burned-out shell. I suppose I hoped it would speak to me, tell me its secrets. But the mutilated remains leaned in silence against the rickety shed.

15 · Intentions and Revelations

It was January 1996. I was fifty-one years old. Still a child. Still running. I wanted to be well or I wanted it over.

The not-so-little bag of coloured pills, my escape from life, still sat in the back corner of the closet where I had found refuge so many years ago, with my candy and my imaginary monkey friends. The nine-month period after Mom's death could well have ended my life. I needed a reason to hang on.

I was unaware that I'd arrived at a fork in my path. There were signs—not billboards or flashing neon, but intuitive warnings. And if there had been signposts pointing in both directions, one of them would have been a skull and crossbones.

There was no one left to fuss over. At the nursing home I'd been a nagging advocate for Mom, always demanding the best for her. But it never occurred to me to do the same for myself. I was gravely ill and bereft of spirit. I could not have known that my desperation would soon be so complete, so utterly perfect, that I would find myself prepared for the next challenge. I felt like a vessel that had been opened to receive a sacred gift. I am deeply beholden to desperation for that very reason.

One day a voice cut through the air, dense with despair. It must have come from my yearning-place. It was my heart, calling out plaintively for a little peace and self-respect. "Pick up that book, sit down, and start reading," it ordered. I heeded that voice. That's what kept me breathing until it was time for the miracle.

I reached for a book on top of the unread pile that had been collecting dust beside my chair. Some I had purchased myself, others had been gifts, and three had appeared in my mailbox at different times with no card or letter of explanation. The book on top of the pile was *Seat of the Soul*, by Gary Zukav.

I could feel the concepts in that book resonating with some place deep within me. They jolted me from my sleepless nightmare. As I read, my ember fired. Shivers shook me, and perspiration beaded on my forehead. The message was clear. Although I had unintentionally created an ugly reality for myself, if I were to seek consciously and purposefully to restore my life, I would be able to do so. My most extravagant imaginings could not have prepared me for what was to begin that day.

Intrigued and invigorated, I remained sober for four days. Sleeping only a few hours at a time, I dove into the books. Poring over the first two books of *Conversations with God*, by Neale Donald Walsch, and *The Dancing Wu Li Masters*, by Gary Zukav, I learned that not everything in the universe is physical. The universal energy that flows through my consciousness produces thoughts and feelings that in turn give form to that energy, and thereby create what I call my life.

The notion that it is possible, by altering my consciousness, to rearrange the energy that courses through me confronted that killing notion that I couldn't get well, that it was too late for me. If I am sad and wish to be joyful, I can confront my sadness by consciously choosing joy. That I can actually *choose* how I feel sounded bizarre to me, but I read on. I learned that by confronting and choosing I can set up different feelings, which will produce different thoughts, which in turn will result in different actions, and eventually my sadness will change to joy. The idea that my thoughts actually create my reality cut sharply into my reverie of hopelessness and denial. It was all starting to make sense.

I felt a pounding in my chest. I realized that it was hope, and it was generated by the possibilities I could see in these new ideas. There was no room for doubt or skepticism. I had to believe. My life depended on it.

According to what I was reading, I create my experience by continually making decisions about the world around me. If I make a choice, or "set an intention," to replace my sadness with joy, my life might not change right away; but if I make my choices carefully, and consciously set my intentions, my attitudes will eventually mirror my choices. This was the most empowering concept I'd ever been exposed to. As I read ravenously about the principles of spirituality and the mechanics of the universe, I was able to see how these things have affected my life. My acceptance of these concepts set in motion a chain of events that altered the direction of my path. One turn of the kaleidoscope and everything in my belief system had changed. It was as if a seed had absorbed just enough water to send out its first sprout.

As I sat in my chair, stunned by the truth on the pages, my eyes shifted to the carpet. I'd been vomiting blood again, and sometimes I couldn't make it to the washroom. The crimson splotches on the walls and floor warned me that I must either believe or succumb again to hopelessness. For weeks I'd been afraid to open the blinds for fear someone might see what I had become. Now I longed for the sun to stream in the windows and for visitors to come through the door. I craved connection to my family, friends, and neighbours.

Other familiar cravings vied for attention. Doubt, fear, and full-body tremors created a powerful thirst for a drink, but awareness settled around my shoulders, warming me with its possibilities, and I was able to resist. Hope gave a huge shudder and shifted my belief system. It felt as if a boulder had been rolled way from a cave. Dreams for my future prickled my skin. I got up, opened the blinds, and sat beside the window. The sun warming my face thawed memories of decades of failed attempts. "Maybe, just maybe, I could be happy," I whispered. And then: "I set an intention to be a person who is sober, drug-free, well, and happy."

I wrote down these words and the date.

I understand now that the moment I uttered those words the wheels of change groaned into motion. Intention-setting was the first wellness tool I would use to weaken the clutch of addiction. The suffocating enclosure was weakening.

My shaking subsided somewhat, and my paranoia as well, and I was able to make several trips to the library. Four days of sobriety stretched into a month. I read *Transforming Pain into Power*, by Doris Helge, *The Wisdom of Florence Scovel Shinn*, *Unconditional Life*, by Deepak Chopra, *A Course in Miracles*, by Helen Schucman, the third book of *Conversations with God*, by Neale Donald Walsch, and *The Power Is Within You*, by Louise Hay.

My mind stretched and flexed as I continued to read. My retention was improving, and I loved how it felt to marvel and ponder instead of seeking oblivion. Sometimes I stared at my tea for the longest time, grateful to have a warm cup in my hand instead of a cold glass of rum and Coke.

All the books had a common theme: I am the creator of my life's experience. Although the things that come into my life are not under my control, I can control my reaction to them. How I react becomes my experience. How I see the world becomes my reality. Perception is everything. These wonderful ideas answered many of the questions I had about life.

The notion that I am really in charge, that it is up to me to make choices, erased the idea that my life was hurtling along out of control and I was helpless to stop it. My ember began to glow again. Leaning stacks of books grew up around my chair as I made my way to and from the library.

The change would take some time, though. I hadn't reached my bottom yet.

I was able to stay sober for several months while I was immersed in reading, but in late winter I had a serious bout of drinking, and then several shorter episodes.

One day a friend told me about an emotional-release retreat, a safe haven facilitated by trained staff where, without judge or censor, I could access repressed feelings that were eating away at me. I knew that the sound lived inside me, in that tangle of feelings I had never expressed. I knew I would die if they remained there.

I would have to be sober for the retreat. No alcohol or smoking was allowed on the facility grounds. I knew that if I was using tranquilizers or antidepressants the feelings would stay where they were, so I slowly tapered off alcohol and all medications. I was frightened, because I was sure that the roar would come—but I felt oddly courageous too.

On the drive to the country with my friend, I felt the fear rising, trying to assume its rightful form, trying to become the sound. I felt it pushing against me, probing for an opening. We pulled up in front of the main building, set back from the road in a bucolic setting a short distance from the St. Lawrence River. What am I doing here? What am I thinking? This is crazy! I reached for the door handle but couldn't move. My friend didn't say a word. I remembered the words, and spoke them again, hoping to break the spell: "I set an intention to be well." Then I climbed out of the car.

We spent the first day getting to know one another. There were fifteen of us. Although it was pleasant enough, I was more accustomed to isolation, and I seriously considered leaving.

The facilitators, Mary Elizabeth and Marilyn, explained the process of emotional release. We would share our feelings. We would identify where they came from and what they represented. We would confront them and put them behind us. We would learn that there are no *bad* feelings, that no feeling has the power to destroy us. And most of all we would learn that to feel was to come alive. We would be loved and comforted through each step. We would be safe. Although trusting others was enormously difficult for me, I discovered, to my surprise, that I believed what they told me.

The second day, Mary asked me whom I wanted to speak to. "The bad man and my father," I replied. We decided that Mary would play both roles. First, though, we spoke at some length about each of these men. Why I trusted her to know what to say I don't know—perhaps it was a flash of intuition.

Mary and I stood about ten feet apart. The others were watching as "compassionate witnesses." She put a scowl on her bad-man face. "If you tell anyone, I'll kill Peter and Rusty," she said.

Years of seething anger rose from the heart-crack, through decades-old layers of resistance, and stormed up with the force of a geyser. I tore at that man, blamed him for the loss of my father's love, ripped him apart the way he did me. I beat him down with all the words that had been stuck underneath the candy, the alcohol, the pills. The shame came forth, the fear broke free, and the anger that had never had a voice spilled into the room. All those years I'd carried him on my back while he whipped me forward over the ruins of my life and down into the boiling hole of addiction spewed up from the killing crack.

I paused to catch my breath, then shuddered. It was over. I felt as tired as I'd ever been. Mary held me for a long time. I told her I felt as though a coat of lead had slipped from my shoulders. Embarrassed to see that I'd wet my pants, I left to have a shower. The water washed me on the outside, and the feeling-words, finally set free, scrubbed away some of the anger from the inside. It was a beginning.

At the next session, Mary said she would play the part of my father. "What is it you want to say to him?" she asked.

"I have a question," I said, "and don't give me any of that psycho-babble nonsense."

"I'll be your father, standing here in front of you. Go ahead. Ask your question."

I took a deep breath and the words tumbled out. "Daddy, why did you stop loving me?"

And my father said, speaking through Mary, "Because I stopped loving myself."

I dropped to the floor and grasped my knees for fear I'd break in two, and rocked, rocked. I could feel the hole where my father's love wasn't. I clutched a pillow and buried my face there, smelling his Three Roses shaving cream. I could feel that soft, scooped-out place in his neck, the forever-love place I'd known as a child. I wept for my father, my mountain. And for the first time ever, I cried real tears of compassion for myself.

That night I watched the moon from my bed. The crescent cut-out in the sky reminded me of a smile on my face in a picture taken when I was about four — before *him*, before the roar, before the running, hiding years, before my father couldn't bear the sight of me.

I continued to read every book on spirituality I could find. I felt a powerful urgency I could not explain. It was as if an intelligent force had swept my mind clean of any notions that did not match my intention to be well and replaced them with just the right combination of ideas to allow healing to begin.

It was thrilling to toss aside the destructive notions I had accumulated since my childhood. I realized that a part of me was dying, but it was the broken part that I no longer needed to drag around. As I read, old ideas that had kept me sick and sad perished before my eyes and were replaced with concepts that nourished me. One morning, as the sun rose above the house across the street, I felt as if I'd been cocooned within these pages over the winter, and that in the spring I would emerge as a butterfly.

I had learned how to set intentions, a practice that became a daily ritual. But setting the intention to be well and acquiring a few tools that would enable me to put that intention to work was very different from wanting to live and face life. Ultimately the books weren't enough. I was fifty years old, bereft of self. I was still secretly adding pills to the bag. Soon there'd be enough. I was so tired of the lies and secrets. I knew that my drinking was hurting my family, but I could not stop. I so wanted them to be rid of me. They were my heart, and I was breaking it.

My pretty home was a prison. I was trapped in the past, a mountain of bones piled up around me. My well-practised smile belied the demons within. Again and again I denied my heart, willing to muffle the roar at any cost. I hated being an impostor. I could not bear to face my present situation, and the future looked equally bleak.

I had absorbed the concepts in my books, but I hadn't yet learned how to turn them into happiness. I was a princess turned into a frog who hadn't yet discovered the words to the magic spell. Each new hope disappeared into the vast emptiness of addiction. The wake of my destruction widened, until the frustration and confusion of those who cared about me turned to anger, then avoidance.

I had always been able to blow on my ember a little, to coax the hope-flame to burn for a while. But I was tired of blowing. My lungs were empty. My eyes were closing on my life. There were more than two hundred pills in the plastic bag. But a miracle was in the making. Angels are real, and very smart. Unknown to me, several miles away an angel was waiting for a ride to my house. I'm not sure what the mechanics of angelhood are, but I don't think he knew he was an angel. He certainly wasn't dressed like one. He had a brown and black coat and looked exactly like a Rottweiler puppy.

A friend of my friend Terry had discovered him wandering alone on a busy street with cars honking and whizzing around him. Digger followed him home, but he already had a dog, so he asked Terry if he knew anyone who wanted a puppy. Terry said he knew of someone who might not want one, but surely needed one. He later admitted to me that he had had misgivings, but he felt compelled to bring the puppy to me anyway. I wasn't aware of it, but my intention to be sober was gathering tools.

The day Digger arrived, I was busy swallowing. The new concepts in my beloved books had slowed my drinking and given me hope, but they hadn't been enough to silence the roar. Swishing his angel-tail, Digger bounded into my house and landed in my heart. His charm was irresistible, his energy intense and frantic, much like my own. This four-legged wonder was between three and six months old, as the vet later told me, he already weighed fifty-eight pounds, and—thank goodness—his tail had not been cut off. His sleek coat was black with tan markings, his paws were huge, his appetite insatiable. His snout was a little longer than most Rottweilers', and the expressive flaps that were his ears were in a constant flurry. And something I could see in his glistening eyes suggested he had a broken spirit, just like me.

On our first night together I took him upstairs instead of a drink. Clucking and cooing, I held him in my arms as he lay on his back like a baby. I told him things I wished someone would tell me. He had that soft, puppy smell. I kissed his face over and over and stroked his little head. "I'll look after you from now on," I said. "I'll never let anyone hurt you again. We're a family now. Just you and me. We'll be fine. We have each other now." His eyes shone. He whimpered most of the night and snuggled closer and closer as if he feared losing me, which would be too much for his confused little heart to bear. I whimpered too. I left the light on so he wouldn't be afraid. That night I knew he was an angel in puppy clothing. To this day I cannot fathom how he hides his wings.

He couldn't do enough to please me. He began to fulfill his mission immediately: he became my reason for living until I could find my own. For now, the many changes necessary to accommodate him would create just enough distraction. He was a very smart little angel.

The ground was frozen, but Terry built a temporary fence around the backyard as best he could. The day was blustery cold. Watching Digger prancing about the yard, snorting through the snow with his very handsome snout, kindled a fire deep inside me that has never gone out, even when I have thought it had. With his arrival something strange began to happen. Just looking at him made me feel such tenderness that I wanted to stay well so that he would be cared for.

There were bowls, dog food, leashes, collars, and toys to collect. At the vet he had his shots, blood tests, and several x-rays, and I made an appointment for his neutering. He was a good boy through all the fuss. He acted tough and friendly on the outside, but his eyes told another story.

I haven't had the experience of giving birth to a child. In view of the path my life took, that is a good thing. I do know how it feels, though, to love Digger with such fullness that the fear of losing him bursts my heart wide open, and the thought of life without him creates a boulder in my throat.

Loving another is like saying, "Here is my heart, do with it what you will." When Digger rolls over and exposes his stomach, he is making himself vulnerable to me. I used to think he only wanted his belly scratched, but it appears to be much more than that for him. He is saying, "I trust you with my life. Here is my belly, my most defenceless spot, do with it what you will."

Hearts and bellies were pretty much all we were about back then. We weren't sure what each of us needed from the other, so we offered what we could. In the beginning I wasn't sure I could handle him, and thought seriously about finding him a better home. He'd been through God knows what and needed a lot of attention, and that was interfering with my struggle to silence the feeling noise. I resented that to some extent, not understanding that this was exactly what he was there for. But my love for him soon transcended everything else. When God sent me a puppy it was because God knew for sure that I wouldn't have let that happen for *any* human.

Digger was surprisingly playful and gregarious considering his past, but his first reaction to being addressed was to lower his head as if he had been bad and expected to be punished. If I picked up a broom or spatula he would cower, and he would never walk near anything stick-like or more than a foot long.

When I returned home from an errand, he would run to crouch, trembling, behind the chair in the living room. The vet said this was common behaviour for a dog who'd made a mistake when he was being toilet trained and had been beaten because of it. Lying on the floor beside him, stroking his anxious face and quivering frame, I cooed to him until his fear passed. I sang made-up doggie lullabies and "There, there, everything will be all right" songs.

Maybe I sang to myself too. I do know that lying on the floor together, behind his hiding-chair, we learned to trust one another. Every soft pat and tickle I gave Digger gave a measure of peace to me too. No one can convince me that he did not offer his damaged spirit so that I could mend mine. I think my little angel knew exactly what he was doing. He knew that my needing him was the only thing that would take my mind off my own pain and distract me from my death march.

Digger was a watcher. Even when he pretended not to, he watched. My drinking slowed down considerably after he arrived, but occasionally I had a relapse. He watched how I changed after the liquor delivery man came, how the tears started again and the structure of our days fell apart among the ruins of empty bottles. He watched as I became well for a time and our lives returned to normal, and how, when the same man returned, the painful process began again. He watched it all: the delivery, the tears, the red-splattered walls, and the nights spent prowling through the house in search of myself. He followed me through the rooms, up the stairs, down the halls. Sometimes the only indication I had that I was alive was his cold nose on the back of my bare leg.

One day Digger had had enough. When the delivery man came, the hairs on his back rose like tiny, black bayonets. He seemed calm, but he was transfixed, still as stone. His eyes, purposeful and dark, never left the man. Just before the delivery man man left, Digger walked over slowly and bit him on the hand, drawing blood. Then he backed away a few feet, positioned himself between me and the man, and glared at him threateningly.

I gave the man a towel to clean the blood off with and offered him some antiseptic and bandages. He refused them, seemingly undisturbed by being bitten. I knew he would come again if I asked him to. But I didn't.

§

In the park nearby, neighbourhood dogs and their owners met every day. I'd hoped to take Digger there to play and learn to socialize with people and other dogs, but I knew that as a breed Rottweilers are feared and judged. I knew how that felt. Addicts are judged too. Digger hadn't been with a group of dogs before, and I was unsure how he'd behave. Knowing he'd been hurt by humans, I thought he might lash out. This would also be my first sober, social meeting with my neighbours, and I was worried we would both be shunned.

If Digger had been a cocker spaniel or some other breed that everyone loves, I wouldn't have had the opportunity to move past my own fear of judgment and rejection. He was the perfect dog for me, because he stretched me past my comfort zone to the place where the glorious personal growth begins. Some people shy away when they see him coming down the street. Sometimes they cross over to the other side. Many are wary of addicts too. I'm learning to be compassionate toward those who fear us. It is not us they fear, but their own inclinations toward viciousness or addiction. It seems we are pieces of broken glass that reflect back to others what life might be for them.

I opened my front door and peered up and down the street. I'd put on clean clothes and a little makeup, and I had been careful when I arranged my hair. Digger was wearing his new red collar and matching leash. He'd made a game of it when I wiped his face and brushed him vigorously. We were ready to meet our two-legged and four-legged neighbours.

The winter sun was blazing brightly. Melting ice drip-dripped from the mailbox. My cheeks tingled from the cold. I was surprised how good it felt to be outside. I loved how my feet felt as they squished through the slush on my front walk. The snow was clean and packy, and just for fun I made a snowball and threw it into the air. Digger caught it in his mouth and shook it as if it was his toy. I could see he was puzzled by its disappearance. I made another and another as we played, laughing and barking, full of life and delight in each other.

In the midst of all this activity I was filled with a small stillness, as if a candle had been lit inside me. For a moment I forgot how badly I needed a drink, although to judge from the waves of tremors that began rolling upward from my knees, my body hadn't. I had promised myself to be sober for Digger's first outing, and that was that.

When we got closer to the park, Digger heard the dogs barking and pulled on the lead. His nostrils quivered. Up ahead I saw dog tails wagging like hairy multi-coloured flags, and I saw a few of my neighbours too.

I assumed they knew about me. We hadn't met formally, but I was sure they'd seen the ambulances, the fire truck, the liquor delivery van, and the haunted look on my face. Digger kept looking back to see if I was all right. I think he could smell my fear.

Suddenly the leash slipped from my hand. He broke away and bounded to the park, heading straight for the professor who lived three doors from us. Digger looked up at him for an instant, then aimed a steady yellow stream at his leather brief-case, which was lying on the ground. I froze. There were several seconds of complete silence; then, as if on cue, everyone started to laugh. They all bade us a warm hello, and as they took turns scratching Digger's back, he stole their hearts, one by one.

If Digger hadn't broken the ice, I wouldn't have been able to share my trepidation with them that day. When they inquired after my life, I said, "I'm an alcoholic trying to stay sober, but I'm not having much luck right now." A woman approached me tentatively and confided that she was a recovering alcoholic, and that her dog had been instrumental in her recovery. I had been worried that they wouldn't want us, but instead I felt connection and understanding.

Many of those people are my friends now. Digger and I learned that day that being up front about who we are lays down fertile soil in which to grow new friendships. Now we walk that park daily, and most days Digger makes a new friend. Sometimes I do too. When he is gone, I intend to plant a tree for him along our favourite path. On it will be a bronze plaque that will say, "For Digger, an angel come and gone."

Why do some people and animals become mean and bitter while others do not? Digger was abused, then abandoned, yet I don't know of a gentler dog. I often wonder how he would have turned out if I hadn't taken the time to love his past out of him. And what would have become of me had he not inter-vened? He and I were nearly mortally wounded, but then we were healed by love, a beguiling, insistent force that picked us up and shook the life into us. We held one another up until we could support ourselves. We wrapped our tattered hearts about each other and held on for dear life. How the lives of all creatures intertwine is seen by some as a mystery. I try to keep it simple. You ask for help and it comes. As our lives have become more structured Digger has settled into his protective mode, and he takes his job seriously. We step out into the world together, not knowing what to expect. The new sense of strength and courage that we found in each other becomes stronger as we venture out into the world of other people.

Each day starts with me coming down the back stairs. When I hit the third step, a thumping begins in the front room, and it becomes louder and faster with each step I take. It is Digger's tail swatting the soft couch he sleeps on. It thumps faster and faster, then stops abruptly when I reach the bottom step. He knows that at this exact spot I will peek around the corner, and then I will run to him, calling his name while he wiggles in delight at our game. My face against his, I rub his belly, feeling his sleepy warmth. Many mornings in the early days I was able to refuse a drink because he was there and so pleased to see me.

He lets me keep my face close for a long time. Then slowly and painfully he rolls off the couch, his hips sore now from arthritis—a result, I suspect, of abuse when he was a puppy. I've taken many serious blows to my body too, some resulting from risky behaviour, some from drunken falls, and some from brutal hands.

Digger dances as I prepare his food. This gay shuffle has slowed down lately, but his eyes still shine like amber lagoons. He eats a soupy breakfast of low-fat organic kibble with a large dollop of canned dog stew on top mixed with hot water. His bowl, crown-shaped and painted in gold with rhinestones and pearls, clearly shows who is the undisputed king of our castle. We both eat a large organic salad each day, with cucumbers, romaine, tomatoes, olives, zucchini, and olives drizzled with sesame oil. Digger likes the tomatoes and olives the best.

Our roles of teacher and student alternate quite naturally. The lessons that flow back and forth between us enrich our lives and challenge our unhealed wounds. One day as I sat in our chair, Digger leaned against my legs as usual, his back to me. It was time for his walk. I leaned over and whispered in his left ear, "Car-car, park." So now he frequently leans his 120-pound frame against my leg and moves his left ear as close to me as he can. He hasn't forgotten that moment years ago when I said those words in his ear. He plays this little trick on me daily. He knows exactly what he's doing. As a result of this clever manoeuvre, I walk a few more miles each week.

The first time Digger and I were separated was extremely difficult for me. While on a cruise to Alaska, I would call his sitter every day. She'd put the phone to Digger's ear while I said hello, and he'd bark at my voice. After the cruise, as the cab stopped in front of my house, I wondered if he would be upset with me for leaving him. When I opened the door he came crashing into me, and all the love he'd been saving for two weeks knocked me off my feet.

On the floor, laughing and cuddling our hellos, we cooed and whimpered about how much we'd missed each other. I'm sure if there had been an excitement-meter handy, it would have shown that I was the one who was making the most fuss. When he looked at me with his ears down, wondering if he'd been bad, I stroked and tickled, murmured and hugged that notion right out of his adorable doggy head. We are sure of each other now, but I think that at that moment he had remembered how sad and frightened he had felt when he was abandoned on a busy street one brutal winter day.

When I headed for the stairs he looked at me with his angel eyes, silently pleading, and I knew I would allow him on the bed just this once. He bounded up the stairs and landed there, his tail in a flurry, as if he'd been sleeping there for years. We snuggled in and I wrapped my arms around his massive frame. Just before falling asleep, I remembered our first night together four years earlier.

There is no doubt in my mind that Digger came into my life in response to my wanting to be well. He is a daily reminder to me that the universe is set up so that we are given the tools to help us fulfill our intentions. People blame God so easily for the sadness and sorrow in the world, but I'm convinced that all God does is observe us exercising free will in our own lives. He does not allow bad things to happen. The universe was created with certain laws, and we either use these laws or misuse them, often with tragic consequences. When I think of how Digger helped me become well, I can't possibly doubt that I have the choice as a human being either to create an ugly reality, or to draw healing to myself through intention-setting. After all that has happened, how can I not know with absolute certainty what my God-Self is capable of, and what the God-Force in the universe can accomplish if I just give it permission to reason with my mind and spirit?

Digger showed me many things about myself just by being who he was; his authenticity became my teacher. When I saw myself reflected in his soft, brown eyes, I knew that I was loyal and steadfast—at least I began to entertain the idea that I could be. When he fanned his tail as we played I learned I was able to offer fun and joy to another living thing. His happy wiggling as I reached for his leash showed me that I could bring pleasure and comfort to another. His rolling over in submission when he had been naughty taught me I could be trusted. His taking so long to get in or out of the car because of his sore joints taught me patience and reminded me to care for my own aches and pains.

Digger's feeding times and exercise needs taught me about routine and structure. Sadly lacking in discipline before he came, I established my routine around his needs. I found that there is safety and freedom in a structured life, that such a life draws a circumference within which I can be free.

I'm sure I wouldn't be walking as much if it weren't for Diggs. He leads me through the park and around the city, introducing me to country paths and twisting trails I wouldn't have discovered without him. Now I seek these experiences out. Walking him, I discovered that if I don't exercise daily my joints will seize and the pain will return.

Digger still watches closely. He hasn't forgotten how it was. When I drank, no amount of coaxing could get him onto the chair with me. Even now, when I cry, he comes to check for that rum smell he hates, because he remembers that every time the smell appears, the tears come too. He approaches, but his tail is not wagging. When the smell check is finished and he's sure, he performs his happy dance, a kind of canine boogie where he lifts his legs and wiggles his back end at the same time. His eyes shine and everything around him rattles and rocks.

When I return home, he greets me at the door more enthusiastically than either of my husbands did. He follows me from room to room and watches. When my day has been hard and the pain of the past has returned, he knows. He comes to me and lays his paw on my knee, speaking clearly through his actions. I respond to him in the second language I've acquired since his arrival, a mixture of baby talk, cooing, and silly, soft noises.

Digger's devotion builds me up and stretches me wide, lifting me to a place of self-care I couldn't have reached without him, a place where shame and bitterness become joy, and I can hardly recognize myself. He helps me take another step forward when I'm worn out from trying. He shows me every day that love can mend a fractured past.

In therapy I was warned that I had become overly dependent on Digger because of my mistrust of people. Tucked away in my denial there is a truth about that for me, but I'm not ready to process it yet. I want us to stay pure and innocent, untouched by the codes and structures of the world. And I vehemently reject the "He's just a dog" mentality.

Maybe I want to keep our friendship separate and safe, untarnished by life's shoulds and should-nots. He taught me that I have a mother's instinct, that I would protect him with my life. He is my child and I am his. It is all heart between us. That's just the way it is. I can live with that quite nicely for now.

I can't imagine my life without Digger. When my mind takes me to that place, a pressing pain stops me in my tracks, a punch in the gut that brings back the tears and leaves me empty, leaves me wanting to fill myself up with all those things that used to take away the pain. But Digger was there when I was afraid to go inside myself to find out who I really was and who I could be. He'll be there until I'm strong enough to go on without him. On that day when he is ever so sure I can stand alone, he will leave me, knowing I will miss him, but sure of something else—I'll be using all the gifts he left with me.

His head is on my foot right now. As I feel his breath on my skin, I know I wouldn't be alive to write these words if he hadn't come into my life. He knows that I know he will stay until I am able to face life, until I no longer need to kill my heart in order to muffle the roar.

When that time comes, I hope I can feel the pain without fear, and in so doing I will cherish his memory. I hope that grace will be there to stroke the sore spot and give me strength to feel the sadness. Digger has helped me understand that nothing bad will happen if I just feel the feelings. He has performed his angel duties with honour.

17 · Surrender

You do not have to stand alone against the gale.
Yield and become part of the wind. EMMANUEL

Being alone had an insidious way of playing tricks on my already-compromised sense of myself. I had no mirror to reflect who I was and who I wasn't. If I had been with others, I might have been able to see who I was in relation to them. The images of myself reflected in them would have been more reliable witnesses than those projected by the paranoia of my disease.

In the absence of people in my life, Digger became my mirror. He reflected both what I was, a guilt-ridden shell, and what I could be, a well and happy person, a romping-partner for him. He was my shadow, following me from room to room, watching. If I moved my arm even a few inches, his head would rise up. He was my very own adoring sentinel.

I had had to change my routine to adjust to his needs. Alcohol would make me drowsy and weak, so instead of drinking first thing in the morning—my pattern before he came—I at first confined myself to a codeine and caffeine combination until after his walk. But it wasn't long before I realized that I was fooling myself, that my need to stop the roar was determined to keep me in my place, and would even make use of a puppy if it had to.

Soon the days and nights began to fold into each other. I had a new alarm clock delivered so that I could set feeding times for the two of us. I began to neglect Digger's walks. He lay by my bed, never complaining.

My body's need for more frequent and larger amounts of alcohol would jar me awake with tremors and hallucinations. Suicidal thoughts, each one more urgent, more enticing, broke through the barrier of sleep and infected my dreams. I began to keep a supply of alcohol and sleeping pills beside my bed— a dangerous and increasingly ineffective antidote.

It became difficult to get down the stairs in the morning, so I started bumping down on my rear end, one stair at a time. Knowing that I would be unable to make the trip again for several hours—not until the alcohol took effect and food gave me strength—I would drag a garbage bag full of clean clothes, books, and medication clunk-clunking behind me.

I would fix myself on the toilet, beside which I'd placed a glass of rum and Coke the previous night. Shaking with disgust, I would hold the glass in both hands, force the liquid down one gulp at a time, lose it in a pail, and then gulp it again. I would sit there performing the gruesome ritual until enough of the chemical had reached my brain to stop the sound of my feelings. Once the alcohol stayed down, food would too.

One morning as I waited for the roar to abate, I acknowledged with rare clarity the seriousness of my situation. I was dying. When I looked around my bathroom I remembered the time I visited a slaughterhouse with my father, when he was delivering a moose he'd brought back from a hunting trip. I'll never forget those red-smeared walls, those buckets full of vague red lumps, and the death, everywhere.

Years before, in Toronto, I'd learned that cold-turkey withdrawal from alcohol could bring on a seizure. I had been warned that that could be fatal, so I was afraid to try it again. I'd been able to stay sober for longer periods after Digger came, but when I did go back to drinking and then tried again to quit, I would use tranquilizers. Then when I tried to stop the tranquilizers, the withdrawal from them would be unbearable, so I would go back to alcohol to deal with that.

I hoped it would be different, that I could just have a few drinks to stop the shaking and leave it at that. But I couldn't. What I didn't know then was that one drink would set up a cycle of craving that couldn't be satisfied no matter how many drinks I had. I would throw up several times a day. When I was too sick to drink anymore, I would go back to the medication, and the vicious cycle would begin again.

My bedroom was a dim cave, grim and hushed. It was where we spent most of our time, our hiding place. The only sounds were Digger's movements, my sighing sounds, and my incessant chattering to myself—which may be all that saved me from going completely insane.

It could have been a bright, sunny room. Two large windows looked out over bountiful gardens and limestone walls. Sometimes when it was dark I'd open the venetian blinds a crack. Neighbours performing routine chores seemed like actors on a multi-levelled stage. In a basement, a child huddled over toys in front of a television. Next door on the second floor, a woman took occasional sips from a wineglass while she cooked supper. In the apartment above, a student watered her plants, plucking dead leaves and stuffing them in her kimono pocket. They seemed a galaxy away.

Mountains of garbage bags full of empty bottles loomed against the walls, gradually filling the room, until only a winding path led from the door to the bed. The pungent odours of urine-soaked sheets and vomit-stained clothing were testament to my inability to care for myself.

Digger was patient. He seemed content to be cuddled, scratched, and sung to instead of having his walks. The truth was I was too afraid to take him out anymore. I had to hide so that no one would see what I'd become, a half-mad prisoner in my own home. A cage with an open door is still a cage.

When Digger first came, I was certain that I'd get better. That I couldn't gnawed at me. He would look at me with his eyes full of trust and love, and it would disgust me that I couldn't walk him. I learned later that there was a flaw in that line of thinking. If my only reason for making an effort was to make someone—or some puppy—love me more, I was bound to fail. I had to want to do it for myself. But I did not yet understand that my disease was a devious, vicious stalker. It was after my life, and my love for Digger was no match for it.

My connection to the outside world was a series of deliveries. Groceries, alcohol, prescriptions, videos, magazines, and dog food would appear by way of the front door. My well-practised smile would greet each arrival: I hoped I wouldn't throw up as I signed the cheques. I hated my life.

This continued for a year. The despair swallowed me up in great, greedy gulps. I felt more and more guilty about Digger. Once again I seriously considered finding him a better home. But he seemed content to wait; after all, he was an angel and knew things I didn't. He would always get up and come to me when he heard my tears, even if he was eating. He'd put his paw on my leg and look up, his eyes glistening-soft, never judging.

Every day I promised myself that this would be the last day of my drinking. I fell on my knees in a vain attempt to strengthen my commitment, and leaned against the bed, one arm over Digger's back. I promised God and myself that today would be different. But eventually my words became like dried leaves on my tongue. I stopped my kneeling ritual. It hurt too much to fail every day.

A year after Digger's arrival, two friends on the same day mentioned the name of a doctor who specialized in addiction. That morning my walls had again been painted in red. I picked up the phone. There were no openings for months, but I went in to register anyway. A few weeks later there was a cancellation, and in the spring of 1997 I met the only human ever to reach me.

§

As I listened to Dr. Hajela, something strange happened. Leaning forward in the chair, my fists clenched, my heart surprisingly open, I actually heard what he said. He spoke my forgotten dreams for me. I'd lost my voice. The alcohol, the drugs, and all the other things I'd swallowed over the years had pushed it down to where words are lost, into the silence of denial, down, down into the voiceless place of addiction.

He spoke words my memory had forsaken, lovely words like "freedom," "honesty," "self-respect," and "fellowship." He spoke those words slowly, carefully emphasizing each one as if for some strange reason it should apply to me. He talked about commitment, discipline, responsibility, and choice, of families mending and hearts smiling, of love, honour, and serenity. His words reached a place I'd hidden from myself, a place so untouched by time and memory that my body shook from the hope of it. He spoke of surrender, the path that would lead me into recovery.

His intuitive presence, his deep spirituality, and his blunt honesty greatly affected me, and I believed him. He wouldn't let me lie to myself, and repeatedly corrected my flawed perception of myself and the events of my life. After this first meeting with Dr. Hajela, I felt an almost imperceptible shift. Was it my shoulders? What was happening in that shame-hunched part of my body? Was my grand height remembering a place it should take my body? How was it possible that the answer lay in surrender?

It would be several months before my last drink and my last drug. But now I had new recovery ideas to go with the spiritual concepts I'd gleaned from reading.

To me, the recovery process was much like a buried gem that was waiting to be mined, cut into brilliant facets, and polished with reverent strokes. But I had to pick up the shovel myself and turn the first piece of earth. No one else could take that step for me. Dr. Hajela made it clear that how all this turned out would be entirely up to me. But he ignited my ember.

When I left his office, I carried a list of suggestions that included attending AA meetings. The memories of my first AA meeting, and tumbling down the steps after being raped and beaten, hurled themselves at me. You can imagine my horror when I realized that one of the things I had to do was walk through the doors of AA again. I had to do it—for Digger.

I pulled into the parking lot in front of the church where the meeting was to be held. There were at least a dozen cars there already. Well-dressed people with smiling faces stood on the stoop. I couldn't imagine what they were so happy about, and resented their heartfelt hellos and solid handshakes. I entered the basement meeting room weighed down by decades of failure, certain there was no other way for me to be, and convinced that it was only a matter of time until I met a tragic end.

That day I learned that there was a life waiting outside my blood-spattered cage. "Do you want to be happy, joyous, and free?" they asked. According to them, there was hope in every fractured heart.

But there was something I had to do first.

A woman offered to be my sponsor. I despised her. She seemed serene and content, and I resented that. We made plans to meet in the coming week to talk about surrender, the first of the twelve steps in the Alcoholics Anonymous program. Conflicted again, I dreaded it, and yet I couldn't wait.

She asked me to think about admitting that I was powerless in relation to my addiction to drugs and alcohol; she asked me to consider that my life was unmanageable. She suggested that I consider surrendering. I couldn't understand how that could have anything to do with my getting well. After all, if I wanted to win, I had to fight, didn't I? I couldn't fathom the notion that surrender and failure were two different things.

I thought I'd fought a good fight. Over the years I'd been to four twenty-eight-day rehabilitation programs and admitted myself to thirty-two hospitals. I had attended twenty-three detoxification programs at the local dry-out facility. There were involuntary admissions too, those fearful, grasping times when I frantically tugged my mind back, although it seemed determined to be lost.

I'd researched and studied for years to find out what vitamins and herbs would build up my body and take away the craving. I had tried hypnotherapy, hydrotherapy, psychotherapy, colon therapy, laser therapy, light therapy, and primal-scream therapy. I had visited countless doctors in countless cities and attended five intensive emotional release retreats. After all that I couldn't just give up, could I? Wasn't that what surrender was—giving up?

The next week Digger and I sat in our chair waiting for my sponsor to arrive. I remembered how most of my life I'd bobbed on a sea of relentless longing for something, anything, to stop the noise. But that day there was something else I longed for. I was tired of fighting, tired of living each day in hell. I wanted out of bondage.

I wanted peace.

Or death.

But I believed Dr. Hajela and the other recovering people I'd met. I had to surrender, they said. There was no cure, no easy way to get better. Instead of fighting a battle I couldn't win, I had to lay down my armour so that I could pick up the tools of recovery.

The many times I'd stopped drinking on my own, nothing had really changed except for the means I used to stop the feelings from coming. There were other things that would do the job besides alcohol. Sober times were only dry times; my thinking and behaviour were unchanged. I may have been sober, but I was still an open wound. I was only putting off that time when I'd reach for something to soothe the decades of unexpressed feelings. I had been told many times that quitting drinking and drugs was the easy part of recovery: the real challenge was learning how to face life without them.

Aware of the sour smells that clung to me, I felt as tired as I'd ever been. I wanted to lie down on the floor and disappear into the cracks. I was so tired. I had tried to get the blood off the carpet and clean myself, but I was too weak. I hadn't had a drop to drink that day. Powerful tremors shook me, and I hung onto my chair and prayed for the strength not to medicate myself. I had something that would stop the effects of withdrawal, a big, bursting bag of it hidden in the closet, but somehow I knew that this was a day for courage.

That knowledge must have been a divine message flung up from some place of self-love that I had abandoned long ago. I clung to it for dear life. The fear and panic were still there with me, close and suffocating. The idea that I wouldn't be able to stop the roar terrified me. The prospect of living in my mind without any escape was unthinkable. Even more frightening was the thought of living the rest of my life that way. Did I really have a choice? Could I try one more time?

Before my sponsor arrived, I had a long talk with Digger, all muddled up with tears, asking him things, telling him things. As I gazed at him intently, hoping to find an answer in his "I love you no matter what" eyes, I felt something shift inside me. I became so absorbed in what I was hearing that I slid off the chair. I strained to grasp what flowed from his heart to mine.

"I understand," I said to him. Taking his soft, whiskered face in both my hands, I looked deep into his soft brown eyes. "Thank you." I kissed his sweet, loving face, and scratched his ears way up inside, just the way he liked it. He wiggled with delight, happy he'd been successful in this phase of his mission.

It was as if a tiny crack had appeared in the distortion of my disease.

I had to surrender. I had to do it for myself.

As I sat in my chair, with Digger pressed close, I noticed the beads of condensation on the handsome eight-foot by ten-foot window. They scurried down the pane helter-skelter, pausing for a second then heading off in another direction, zigzagging fitfully. Their wet trails left little maze-paths on the glass. I felt connected with the droplets of water. I knew what it was like never to know where I was going, how I'd got there when I arrived, or in what direction the next moment would take me.

As I waited, a voice spoke to me, a long-forgotten voice that came from a place inside that hadn't yet been ruined, a place my heart kept as a kind of back-up when all appeared to be lost. That was where, if I was well enough to remember to look, I'd find that small breath to blow on my ember. For a reason that could only have been divine, I listened. I got up from my chair. Digger got up too.

Then, something curious happened. Digger cocked his head as if he was hearing something special too. Even in my stinking, shaking state, I knew this to be a moment of supernatural intervention. I'll never forget the tingling that spread across my shoulders. It was as if a legion of wings were pressed against my back, and a choir of heavenly voices were singing me forward. I felt Digger's breath warm on the back of my leg. Together we marched nearer and nearer to the closet that held death's rainbow. The celestial music overwhelmed the roar and lifted me over the last few feet. We arrived at the closet, the same closet that had been my hiding place when I was a child. In one last attempt to face life, I reached for the bag of little coloured pills.

Knowing they were there had been a comfort. I knew that whenever the roar finally became too much to bear, they would take me away to a peaceful place, a silent place. Now Digger and I marched to the bathroom and flushed death down the toilet. I'd chosen to live. There was no escape now.

I felt utterly bereft. I was left with no defence against the sound.

The doorbell rang. It was my sponsor. She looked fresh, sparkly, and too darned sure of herself. Her long blonde hair was neatly held in a pretty tortoise-shell barrette, and her clothes were trendy, clean, and pressed. When she smiled her nose didn't twitch, even though I knew I smelled. The odour of a desperate life didn't seem to bother her. I was embarrassed to feel the strings of spittle running down my chin. I couldn't stop them. I couldn't speak.

I'd hit bottom.

"Nancy, you can't do this on your own," she said. She touched my wet face with gentleness and leaned toward my stinking body to hug me. "Let someone help you."

After having struggled my own way for forty years, I knew that the only way had to be a way other than my own. My head was hanging, but not in embarrassment. My shoulders were rounded, but not in shame. As I'd watched the pills swirl away, I'd taken my first real step. Dishevelled, reeking, in front of a woman I couldn't stand, I learned what humility was.

I had surrendered.

Because I was so ill, and needed badly to lie down, I did not encourage her to stay. She handed me some literature and suggested I get to a meeting as soon as possible, which I assured her I would. I walked her to the door and stood there as she got into her car.

I felt as though a veil had been lifted to reveal what I had been searching for my whole life long: peace. I no longer had to do it my way. I didn't have to lose. I didn't have to fail. I didn't have to fight anymore. By giving up, I had won. By giving in, I had empowered myself. By reaching out, I'd saved myself from myself. I'd swallowed the last of my little coloured pills. I'd drunk the last drop from the glass that was my life.

I looked up and down that street where thousands of my footprints lay invisible on the cement. The laneways were still there, the same ones I had raced through, seeking a place to hide from the bad man. The ghost of my child self still travelled through the backyards and over the fences, looking for a resting place. Across the street was the house with the dark rooms.

Maybe I didn't have to run anymore.

It may sound strange, considering my past, but the first several years of recovery were the most difficult of my life. I was entirely conscious: no more sleepwalking, no more drowsy heart-dead stumbling in a fantasy world, no more eyes-open blindness. If I was to be well, there would be no more skipping the sad parts of life or the bad memories, no more playing hooky from the real world.

Seventy years ago, the founders of the Twelve-Step philosophy discovered something that transcended the variables of time and human nature. Not just some, but all those who follow the twelve steps exactly will experience certain transformations—which they called "promises."

I was assured a freedom and a happiness I had never known. I would feel no guilt about my past—nor would I try to forget it. I would reach a truce with my past; I would neither forget it nor feel guilty about it, I would simply accept it for what it was. I would understand fully what serenity is, and find a peace I never thought possible. I would learn how to handle situations that used to confuse and frighten me. I would learn how to replace my mistrust of others with acceptance and discernment, and my unproductiveness with a sense of purpose. Instead of feeling sorry for myself, I would accept responsibility for the outcome of my life. No longer interested only in myself, I would start to care about others and the world I lived in. I would believe at the deepest level that no matter how far I had fallen, my experience would be useful to others.

These changes would weave their wonder through my life only gradually. I would still have fears, but I had tools of recovery now, and no longer needed to seek escape through alcohol or drugs. I finally understood that the only way to silence the roar was to face it—to face life.

Quitting alcohol and drugs was the easy part. The transformation part the founders talked about was the hardest thing I ever did. Decades of resentments, guilt, blame, self-pity, shame, and fear that had served my addiction long and well were resistant to change.

My ember grew to a licking flame. It scorched my heels and made me dance a frantic jig of remembering: not the false, distorted memories produced by denial or selectivity, but memories of the truth as it really happened. Layer after layer of betrayal, bitterness, and victimhood burned and peeled away, revealing sore after festering sore.

I had my last drink on January 1, 1998, and took my last drug at the end of that February. My "clean date," then, was established as February 28, 1998. Raw and frightened, I understood how crucial it was to have a structure that would support the work I needed to do to rid myself of all the traits and behaviours I'd collected over the years as defences against my pain. If all I did was stop using and made no other changes, I'd just be a sick person who happened to be dry. By admitting my powerlessness over drugs and alcohol, by surrendering to this incurable disease, I would empower myself to manage it successfully. The Twelve-Step philosophy is an instruction manual, a guide through the recovery process; it has been proven and tested by time. It provided me with a structure within which I knew freedom for the first time. The essence of that philosophy is surrender—it was surrender that I experienced when Digger and I watched the bulging bag of pills being flushed out to sea.

In the months following that day, many things became clear. Addiction is an incurable disease and I am utterly powerless against it. By surrendering, I freed myself from the unwinnable battle I had enmeshed myself in. By laying down my armour I conserved the strength I needed in order to lift up the tools of recovery. I came to understand clearly one of the truths of nature: what I resist persists. I would have to learn how to embrace my disease, to come to know it so well that I could partner with it in becoming well. If I were to admit my powerlessness over drugs and alcohol, if I were to surrender to my disease, I would be free from the muck I'd been trudging through.

But that was only the beginning.

A friend of Peter's once asked me why I needed to be in a recovery program. Why couldn't I just stop drinking and leave it at that? I explained that drinking was only a symptom of a much deeper problem, the root of which was a faulty wiring of the brain, which caused a skewed perception of events, traumatic or otherwise. That flaw prevented me from coping with life in a healthy way. The addictions came later, as a symptom of my frustration with my inability to cope with the consequences of a life lived in chaos. Then the disease of addiction, which has at its command a vast assemblage of devices, used those consequences as reasons to continue drinking. So stopping my drinking and drug use was the easy part. It would provide me with the mental clarity to tackle the hard part—learning how to cope with life without them.

Today I am joyful beyond measure. I care for and about myself, and embrace my life with uncensored delight. I am a hundred and fifty pounds lighter, a non-smoker, and scrupulous about what does and doesn't go into my mouth. Now I am able to walk through the streets of my town with my head held high. It wasn't so long ago that shame kept my head down, and my neck aching from its weight. Remembering is good if it's done with acceptance and gratitude.

Following the twelve steps provided many blessings. I looked forward to most of them, but there were three that I dreaded: the moral inventory, sharing that with another person, and making amends to those I had harmed.

The only way to find the truth was to view my past through the lens of recovery. Only then could I deal with the mind monsters, those fifty-year-old memories twisted by guilt, blame, resentment, shame, and sorrow. Once I knew the truth I could understand it, accept it, and let it go. That was the key to long-term sobriety and sanity. That was the path to freedom.

Recovery is a filling-up time. But I had to empty out first. To do that, I had to confront every one of my lying, thieving monsters. In recovery language it's called a "fearless moral inventory." I had a choice. I could move through the fear and face my past, or spend the rest of my days only superficially changed —dry but still sick, existing but not really living. I wanted it all: the heart-dancing, wide-grinned, jumping-up and heel-clicking kind of freedom. I would be just as relentless and ruthless in my healing as I had been in my efforts to silence the roar.

But I couldn't fix what I couldn't see. My disease and I, master masons, had been frantically cementing a wall of habitual, unhealthy ways of coping for decades. This wall had to come down, brick by brick. Only then would I be able to see it all: the misguided need to control everyone and everything, the misdirected anger and blame, the sadly sophisticated victimhood, the self-pity, the all-or-nothing thinking, the irrational fear, the grandiosity, the resentments, the dishonesty, the jealousy, the self-loathing, and the begging for approval—all those defences against the pain and shame and dreadful secrets that gave addiction a foothold. All those tools I'd collected to create the illusion of safety.

That "fearless moral inventory" took months to complete. I made a list of every single episode in my life that gave the roar its thunder. I remembered them as they really happened, not as addiction would have me remember them. Each incident was scrutinized, itemized. I broke the lead of countless pencils and the nibs of countless pens. For each incident I doggedly identified whether it was arrogance, fear, anger, guilt, or the need for approval that motivated me. The inventory empowered me to accept ownership of the part I played and to take responsibility for the carnage that had been my life.

Gradually my frantic running slowed to a trot, then to a walk, until one day I turned around and faced the sound. The roar, which I now knew was only yesterday's bully, was reduced to a squeaking coward. It was like a cockroach that scurries away when the light comes on. It was about to take its rightful place in that remote corner where I keep my painful memories.

Only truth could reason with that memory. Only by reflecting on each bit of my life could I see the past as it really was.

I dissected and inspected resentments; I sought out immoral behaviours, one by guilt-ridden one. There must be nothing left to beckon the roar. Sobriety depended on my ability to be honest. This step of recovery represented the growing edge of life-changing, life-giving sanity. And it held a promise. Powerful in its catharsis, it would reveal the decent person that had been buried under a heap of hideous secrets.

§

Today I would take the next step. I slammed the car door and started the engine. My foot, heavy with trepidation, rested like a rock on the gas pedal. The wheels spit gravel at the garden fence.

It was a twenty-minute drive along the lake to my twelve-step sponsor's home. Today Shirley would hear about every wrongful deed I could remember ever having committed. A mist had drifted over the highway from the marsh, and it swirled behind the car. The earthy smell wafting in the windows reminded me of the way Dad smelled after hunting, when he stood at the kitchen door grinning, holding a bag of ducks.

Beside me on the car seat were notebooks containing 235 events, my moral inventory. I had turned these events into written words, so the past was no longer inside me—but they were still secrets, and therefore still powerful and poisonous. Today I would disclose each of those events to Shirley, every heart-cracking one of them, and discuss their exact nature with her. I wouldn't move on to the next one until I fully understood my role in each and the consequences of my actions.

As I pulled into the driveway, I asked for the strength to leave nothing out, to tell the truth to another human being for the first time. I sat for a moment looking at the wall of railway ties supporting Shirley's garden. Feisty little green shoots tucked in and out of the wooden crevices. The wall reminded me what I was here to do. I had come in order to demolish the old walls that keep the past alive inside, cause the present to fester, and restrict the future. I came in order to stop the sound. A train whistled by on the tracks behind me and I chuckled at another metaphor. I was the train, and the tracks were the recovery process. I had to stop here to deposit the baggage of the past if I wanted to reach my destination—freedom.

Shirley met me at the door with an easy smile and a long hug. I was trembling, but she'd been through this too and understood my fear. The teakettle was whistling like the train, and I felt safe. Spring sunlight slanted through the blinds, laying down golden ribbons on the carpet. Her home was soft and peaceful, and many memories were hanging on the walls. Faces in wooden frames smiled down; some had never known the hell she'd been through.

I opened the first of my notebooks. It was all there, the roar's devastating effect on my life, scribbled frantically over many months. Having learned to adore the truth, I told Shirley everything. I didn't justify my actions or point the finger at anyone else. It all poured out, the words tripping over each other, grateful to escape the slaughterhouse inside. She nodded encouragement, knowing exactly where, and why, I was faltering. There's a certain look I'd seen on people's faces all my life, but it did not appear on hers. She had been there too. The pain was the same, only the details were different.

Fear, anger, and guilt tumbled out. When exposed to the light, the decades of dishonesty, unfair judgment, immoral and approval-seeking behaviour dissipated like cowardly phantoms. By being honest, I was able to transform feelings of resentment, jealousy, and blame into simple regret. That day Shirley was as direct in her responses as I was in exposing my past. Just the truth, clean and sharp. After speaking to her for several hours, I finally forgave myself for being human.

I was surprised to notice that I tiptoed away from Shirley's stoop. I closed the car door gently, reverently, as if respecting the fact that I'd taken part in the divine order of things. I needed to be quiet for a time, so as not to disturb my serenity. I felt strangely soft and hollow, as if a malignant growth had been removed. My eyes, free at last, searched every corner of my life, but found there was nothing left to feed the roar. I'd wiped the slate clean.

On the way home, I thought of Digger. I couldn't wait to tell him what freedom felt like. I always told him everything. He was such a good listener. He'd cock his head this way and that, his amber eyes glistening, his tail swishing its giant swash. I thought, I'll tell him that it felt like being lifted by warm golden air to the very spot I'd always dreamed of. I could see my past from there as a garment rich and fiery-bold, and its threads appeared to be unravelling. As the last filament fell away, all the faces from all my yesterdays faded from view. Only their hard lessons remained, as a truth fine and good to build my future upon. Freedom would lend me the grace to hold that garment sacred and to view its tapestry from time to time — and the wisdom never to have to be clothed in it again.

Driving home along Lake Ontario, I pretended that the massive waves were clapping against the shore in celebration, and the gulls were calling after me, "Truth, freedom, joy." The poplar trees on the sides of the road bowed, honouring my willingness to face life. The world of pretend is an enchanting place to visit, but I'm grateful not to have to live there anymore.

I whipped into the back lane behind my house and jumped out of the car. I had an idea. Digger pranced, wiggled, and wagged his angel tail as I gathered up the notebooks, placed them in a metal pail, and took them into the backyard. I held a match to the corner of a page and stood back. The flames rose: the past became ashes.

I could feel my soul doing a line of perfect cartwheels.

§

In some cases it was years before I realized that a particular resentment was still lurking in my mind, gnawing away at my serenity. Sometimes a betrayal is so old and excruciating it takes all that time to peel back the layers and understand its precise dynamics. Sometimes when humility is absent from this process and I can't or won't see what my part was in the situation, I continue to blame others. By holding on to my resentment toward them I cause myself further pain and anxiety.

My marriage had ended eight years earlier. I thought I had dealt with having been betrayed by my girlfriend, but one day when I was speaking with my former mother-in-law—it was a few months before I began my inventory—I realized that my feelings about the situation were still festering. There had been many layers to that betrayal, each thick with grief, anger, disbelief, and blame. I had accepted my ex-husband's behaviour, having expected it to happen sooner or later, but the seething anger at my girlfriend's premeditated duplicity was different, more complicated. You'd expect to be safe with a girlfriend who quoted scripture and pretended to care.

I hated hating her. I wanted to be free of it. It wasn't until I sorted it out on paper and talked about it with Shirley that I clearly understood my part in the situation. If my judgment hadn't been impaired by alcohol, I'd have made different choices in friends—and husbands, for that matter. I had needed companionship so badly that I was willing to pay for her friendship in money and goods, and I ignored my own intuition and the concerns of family and friends.

I'm not making excuses for myself, but addiction had a way of twisting my mind so that I trusted people I should not have and became suspicious of those who had my best interests at heart. When I humbly accepted my own behaviour, I was able to comprehend that the same fear and shame that motivated me had motivated her. Only our agendas were different. When I drank, I set myself up as the perfect victim, which ultimately coloured my choice of friends. Predators don't usually bother with people who aren't easy prey. I didn't have to condone her behaviour, but when, during my inventory, I explored my own behaviour, I could understand how fear, greed, and shame could drive an otherwise good person to act in such a way.

On my knees, with one arm over Digger's back, I asked my higher power to remove all the resentments that had so efficiently destroyed my peace. I was careful to give particular consideration to this situation. I finally took responsibility for my part in it. I stopped blaming her and shed the victim role.

When I think of her now, I feel truly sad that she lived in such fear and unworthiness that she was compelled to commit those acts against her own humanity. It was herself she hurt so badly. The poison that she infected herself with simply ricocheted onto me because I put myself in its way.

With Digger close, I asked for the strength to embark on a journey of oneness with the world, to join the process of life and begin to trust it. I no longer felt set against life. As I left the old and embraced the new, I breathed in a perfect moment of grace—and I exhaled my old friend's betrayal.

§

The step I dreaded perhaps more than any other was making amends to those I had harmed. The list was a paper graveyard that came alive during my inventory process and rose from my notebooks in a column of frightful spectres. There were so many on my list, and I expected most of them to spurn me. Sometimes, though, the harder the task, the greater the reward.

Living in the house where I'd grown up, I frequently saw a man who'd owned one of the many small stores in my neighbourhood that had a candy counter. He was elderly now but his eyes were still kindly, as I remembered them.

I'd stolen candy from his store for years. Licorice babies, mint leaves, gumdrops—I'd grab what I could, hide it in my pockets, and race home to stash it in my hiding closet. I stole from other stores too, but mostly from his, because he always seemed to be looking the other way.

Now I felt guilty whenever we happened to pass each other on the street. But he always had a smile for me. He would occasionally stop and ask how I was, and always seemed particularly interested in my answer. I wondered about that.

One Friday morning when I stepped out of my door I saw him walking along spryly on the opposite side of the street. I can recall the scene with amazing clarity. Further down the street heavy equipment was installing new water pipes before winter, and it heaved and rumbled. A clay pot of die-hard geraniums sat on my neighbour's front step and a hint of summer lingered in her garden.

My feet must have known something I didn't. They stepped purposefully onto the road and headed toward the man I'd stolen candy from so many years ago. I approached him with my head down, still ashamed, still very much the little thief.

"Hello, Nancy," he said, in his usual pleasant but serious way. "How are you today?"

He wore a light-blue plaid shirt and navy cotton pants with perfect creases. Wiry white hair poked out around his ears.

I ignored his question. "I have an apology to make to you. I stole a great deal of candy from your store when I was young. I'm really sorry. I just wanted to tell you that."

Now he looked at the ground too, for what seemed like forever. His eyes had changed to sad and ashamed, just like mine. He spoke softly, slowly, as if he was tired. He seemed a bit stooped, like someone who had been carrying something heavy on his back for a long time.

"I knew you were stealing candy," he said, his foot moving a twig this way and that. I could tell he was self-conscious, but couldn't understand why. "I let you have the candy because of the look in your eyes. It hasn't changed much."

I broke into a sob right there on the street, with the traffic whizzing by, the jackhammer pounding, and the neighbour peeking out her kitchen window. I held my hands over my face to cover the shame. I blurted it all out to the old man. I told him about the bad men and how the candy made me feel better.

I didn't intend to. As I spoke, tears steamed down his cheeks and his mouth quivered. He stopped moving the twig and looked me right in the eye. For a moment I thought he was angry with me.

"I knew," he said, the words having a hard time getting past his tears. "I knew, and I couldn't help you. So I let you have the candy."

His body started to shake, in little quakes that grew to man-trembling weeping that years of conditioning tried to subdue. He and I must have looked a sight on the street, crying away the years of secrets and guilt, at long last having the chance to speak our regret, so unexpectedly and with such uncensored humility.

I grabbed his arms and held on firmly, to make my point more clearly. "It's okay." I said, "It's in the past. I just wanted to say I was sorry."

"No, Nancy," he said with equal determination, "*I'm* sorry."

We hugged, each of us realizing that we had received a gift, neither of us having expected gifts at all.

§

Truth and honesty in all things have given me freedom; it hovers over my life like a shining star. I know well that a return to bondage is only one lie, one deceitful act away, but I sometimes feel that I've grown wings that will carry me through my life with gladness and honour. What more could I want than the freedom to soar, unencumbered by guilt and shame? The key was to allow myself the option. And the allowing came with my surrender.

§

Now, with wonder and gratitude, I breathe in my hopes and dreams. I inhale deeply and my spirit is replenished. Neither foul weather nor a surly disposition can cause me to miss more than a beat or two. I squeeze life into every day and can't wait to start another. I can't smile widely enough to show how it feels to have a second chance. But there are no restrictions to the width of heart-smiles.

The crack is nearly mended.

Freedom for me has meant facing life, viewing the landscape of my days with both feet planted in reality. No escaping into a world of rosy veils, pretty pills, or potions laced with denial. Just life, both sweet and ugly. Sweetness may grant a fleeting tickle of the senses, but ugliness—now there's fertile ground for cultivation of the spirit.

A year into recovery, I sat across from my doctor while she shared with me the fact that recent tests showed I had active hepatitis C, as well as late-stage cirrhosis of the liver.

"Have you had a blood transfusion?" she asked.

"Many years ago now."

"When exactly?"

"In the early eighties." I told her about my suicide attempt and the blood transfusion that saved my life.

"That's when the Red Cross had all that trouble with bad blood. Thousands of people were infected with hepatitis and HIV and weren't aware of it. It's all coming out in the open now."

"Ironic, isn't it?" I muttered, more to myself than to her. "I knew something like this was going to happen." A few months earlier I'd shared with my recovery group a feeling of doom that had been lurking beneath my success in achieving sobriety. Ever since my last drink I'd been plagued with worry: now that I'd found some measure of peace and happiness, a serious medical condition resulting from decades of substance abuse would surface. According to the test results, that anxiety had actually been a premonition.

I left the doctor's office shaken and frightened, but took comfort in knowing that Digger would be waiting. I needed to talk it through with him before I told anyone else. He met me at the door with his usual uncensored enthusiasm, and noisily chomped his carrot while I made a cup of tea.

We settled into our chair and I prayed for the strength to resist falling into the unhealthy, deeply entrenched patterns of coping—fear, blame, denial, shame, anger, and self-pity.

The answer to my prayer came swiftly and with great clarity. As Digger's solid bulk warmed me, I realized that my recovery work had prepared me for a day such as this. For me, spirituality has nothing to do with religion. It is a belief in something greater than myself and a profound sense of the interconnectedness of all living things. Many opportunities for spiritual growth had come to me over the years; but I didn't recognize them, because they were disguised as ugliness. That afternoon I fully understood that my continued wellness depended on my developing the capacity to accept circumstances that might at first appear to be ugly. And more than anything, I had come to know that everything happened for a reason, for the greater good in my life, no matter how contrary the evidence seemed at the time.

I could choose to perceive the hepatitis as an ugly thing, and draw more ugliness into my life in reaction to that perception. Or I could choose to see it as an opportunity. The gift of spiritual growth would occur when I was able to admit to my fear —terror, actually—of being sick again just when I'd become well, and of having to put myself in the care of the medical profession, which I had little respect for and absolutely no trust in. By exposing and acknowledging that fear, I disarmed it. I could then accept it as my present reality, and as my partner in learning how to grow into fearlessness.

Acceptance was always the key, always the challenge. Part of the fear was rational. In the sixties and seventies I had admitted myself into hospitals countless times, hoping for answers, for healing. Mostly they were brutal, unforgiving places, although there were rare and touching exceptions. Little attempt was made to disguise the belief that alcoholics were a waste of time, less-than-human nuisances, a revolving door of fetid smells and tiresome excuses. And a woman alcoholic! Unacceptable! Memories of intentional humiliation, snide comments, and downright physical abuse still hurt. And after six years of visiting Mom in a nursing home, watching people shrivel from borderline neglect and malnutrition of the heart, I had a deep and enduring fear of someday being one of them.

I did not accept my situation right away. Not for months. And I didn't expect to. Some days I was enraged, full of blame and self-pity; the cravings were still powerful, the fear unbending. But that was my process. To deny it would be to fall into the old heart-killing ways. I felt the feelings, I didn't drink, and between the unwavering support of my recovery team and my solid spiritual foundation, I was soon rescued from my stint of "poor-me" thinking.

One of the books I'd re-read just before the diagnosis was *Anatomy of a Spirit*, by Carolyn Myss. It presented to me again, in a most providential way, one of the first life-changing ideas I'd gleaned from my beloved books in the days before Digger came: it would be impossible to stay in a victim mindset if I stopped blaming others for my circumstances. Accepting responsibility for my part, no matter how small, in bringing about those circumstances would move me from victim to survivor. As a result of that tiny crack in my awareness, I realized I could learn, grow, and move on from this experience instead of being stuck in blame. That didn't mean I had to condone bad behaviour or excuse negligence on the part of others; I just had to accept responsibility for my role.

When I'd finished the last chapter of that book, I felt infused with power. With absolute clarity I understood how I'd acted as the perfect victim most of my life. But now I had a choice. It was true I'd received infected blood from a supplier. But it was also true that my own actions had put me in the hospital. I couldn't move forward and see the ugly thing as a gift until I believed that with all my heart.

Believing and knowing are quite different, however. My experience is that believing comes from information, observation, and an understanding that something is possible. Knowing comes from having an experience, a physiological frame of reference that sits in our bodies as cellular memory and cannot be dislodged by a new belief or the latest theory. When my knowing came, it was quite a surprise.

§

On my way to visit my brother and sister-in-law, I thought about not telling them, worried that they'd see this as just another piece of bad news about me that they'd have to deal with. The short trip seemed like a thousand miles to me, still a relatively inexperienced driver, and I was tempted to turn the car around—but I couldn't wait to get there, either.

The day was glorious. Sharp-clear air allowed a perfect view for miles. I rolled down the window, inhaled the sweet smells of the land readying itself for winter, and imagined it pulling the blanket of fallen leaves over itself to hunker down till spring. But there was no prospect of such comfort for me. I was sick with worry that my family might shun me now that I carried the virus. But they deserved to be told and offered a choice.

I finally arrived, with a lump in my throat the size of a basketball. Peter and Ann gave me a tour of their newly built home, and we ended on the patio, where we sat down. As the smoke wound through the stand of sumacs at the end of Peter's driveway I was reminded of my dad burning leaves at the lake property years ago.

We had a fine visit, and at the end of it I summoned up the courage to tell Peter and Ann about the hepatitis C and how I had acquired it. They both listened intently as the words skidded from my tongue. I waited for "the look" to appear on their faces. But it never did.

"Nancy, would you like some more tea?" asked Ann. "I'll put on another pot on if you like."

"Sure," I said, my casual reply concealing how much that simple, spontaneous question meant to me. They didn't seem repulsed by my presence or in a hurry for me to leave. After Ann returned, I continued until I was finished.

With no hesitation, no judgment in his voice, Peter said, "That's a really rotten thing to happen to you. I'm sorry you have to go through this."

Since I hadn't been sure what to expect, Peter's reaction touched me deeply. His words were a cooling salve. In the first stages of our mending process we had approached each other tentatively, so when those words connected with my heart I had an epiphany. The "poor me" attitude that addiction uses so exploitatively suggested to me that I could use this situation to gain attention. I wanted his love and understanding badly, and the real compassion in his eyes tempted me—but I didn't want to be the old me. I wanted our burgeoning relationship to be about honesty. This was an opportunity to change an unhealthy pattern.

I took a deep breath and said, with tears in my eyes, "No, Peter, it didn't 'happen to me'; I brought it on myself. It wouldn't have happened if I hadn't had to be there in the first place. If I blame the hospital, then I'm assuming a victim role. My own hand put me there. I have to take responsibility for that. Besides, it takes so much energy to hold a grudge. I need all my energy for recovery."

I felt the power of those words enveloping me as I drove away. A few miles up the road, I pulled over to write in my journal, not wanting to forget a moment of the encounter. I had been given an opportunity to abandon my habit of casting myself as the victim, and I had done so. I had been able to rise above the self-seeking patterns of addiction. I felt no sense of moral superiority; it just felt good and right.

I found myself wearing a true-to-myself grin and loved the way it felt on my face. The road back home became a golden river, and I flowed gently inward to that divine place where honesty and dignity reside, a place in me that had been long-forgotten, a place where my code of honour dwelt. That day I became a person I could respect.

I began to see that my virus was offering me opportunities to become the person I'd dreamed of being. I hadn't needed to hide the truth in order to secure my family's approval, as I'd done most of my life. I didn't have to abandon my own values to be loved and understood by them. I had a new frame of reference.

The gift was unwrapping itself.

§

According to my doctor, at the time of my hepatitis C diagnosis I was in desperately poor health, and *might* have lived a few years. I was 150 pounds overweight and pre-diabetic. I smoked two large packages of cigarettes a day, ate mostly fatty processed foods, and sometimes consumed pounds of candy at one sitting. My blood pressure was high. Chronic arthritis, depression, hypoglycemia, irritable bowel syndrome, and an enlarged cirrhotic liver were taking a toll.

I was still weak and shaky, still unable to go up and down the stairs when I needed something, still dependent on the garbage bag full of supplies that I brought down with me at the start of the day. Untreated sleep apnea and restless leg syndrome made me chronically insomniac, so I was always desperately tired. Just before my diagnosis, I had worried constantly about how I was going to deal with these physical problems on top of all the emotional, mental, and spiritual demands of recovery. Hepatitis C gave me a reason to tackle it all.

Soon after I was diagnosed, the doctors at the liver clinic strongly suggested that I take a pharmaceutical approach to hepatitis C, a combination of Interferon and Ribovarin. After researching extensively on my own, I learned that severe depression, pulmonary and thyroid damage, auto-immune disease, insomnia, and severe flu-like symptoms were among the many debilitating side effects of such treatment. It would be necessary for me to take the treatment for at least a year, maybe two. Complete and sustained elimination of the virus was not a common response in patients with my particular set of conditions. Because there was only a small chance that the treatment would work, and because I had powerful intuitive feelings about the matter, I decided against it.

A doctor I hadn't spoken to before bluntly expressed her concern about my refusal to accept the recommended treatment. "Nancy, you'll go into liver failure if you don't," she said. I was certain that all the doctors at the clinic had my best interests at heart, but I also knew that doctors were extremely busy, and relied on the pharmaceutical companies to provide information about the side effects of drugs—and that some of these companies had been penalized for not disclosing all the details regarding side effects. I took the time to talk to dozens of people from all over the country who had undergone the protocol. And the news wasn't good. When I researched the study on which the success rates for the treatment were based, I noticed that none of the people in the study who had been made free from the virus had had cirrhosis. Further research revealed that the virus was able to hide from the anti-virus medication in cirrhotic tissue. I was convinced that the odds of the treatment's working in my particular case were poor.

I was in stage four of liver disease. Stage five meant liver failure and death. With the virus aboard, I had to make a choice. The alcoholic cirrhosis had been arrested when I stopped drinking, but cirrhosis is also caused by hepatitis C. My liver disease would continue to progress unless I could find a way to slow it down, and I chose to make that happen by drastic lifestyle changes plus a combination of traditional Chinese and herbal therapies. Now fifty-seven years old, I sensed that I'd ultimately die a natural death from some other cause than liver failure. I had been unhealthy for fifty years, I was feeling as well as I ever had despite my many physical problems, and I had no intention of taking a treatment that would make me sick for two years or longer and had little chance of clearing the virus.

I spent hundreds of hours in the library familiarizing myself with how the liver worked, and what substances in food and the environment would shorten its lifespan and further compromise its function. To extend the life of my liver, I began eating organic food, installed a water-filtration system in my home, used only non-toxic cleaning supplies, and looked at everything that went into my body in an entirely new way.

Actually, I had been researching for years. Back in 1967 I'd read about the Shute brothers and their discovery of vitamin E. I had become obsessed with the idea of finding something —anything—that would make me feel better. I'd spent a great deal of time at that time in the library poring over ponderous medical volumes. At that time I had no idea what was wrong with me, but I suspected I was insane.

For decades I'd known that I was addicted to sugar. My research now revealed that sugar facilitated a more rapid replication of viruses, so I decided to eliminate sugar from my diet entirely, something I had tried to do hundreds of times.

When I joined Overeaters Anonymous, I learned about the abstinence concept. If I wanted to be free of sugar cravings, I had to do what I'd done with alcohol and drugs: I stopped eating sugar completely, as well as foods that changed to sugar rapidly in the body (potatoes, white rice, and anything made with white flour). After five days of withdrawal, the effects of which were similar to but not as severe as those of alcohol and drug withdrawal, my physical cravings for sugar disappeared. The remaining cravings, triggered by emotional stress, could be dealt with by using the tools of recovery. The promise of the Overeaters Anonymous program was simple: the more I faced life, using the tools of recovery, the less the roar would drive me into overindulgence.

Chronic arthritis in all of my joints except my left hip and right elbow begged to be medicated. But because anti-inflammatory medication was toxic to my liver, and narcotic-based drugs were out of the question, I had to find new ways to deal with the pain. My research led me to information about food choices and supplements that offered relief. I didn't enjoy exercise, but I found that yoga and stretching helped the pain immensely, and improved my whole-body health. And the more I exorcised anger, fear, resentment, guilt, and shame, the more I was able to tolerate any remaining discomfort.

In the meantime, one of the liver specialists at my clinic told me that recent tests had identified the precise genome of the virus that I was infected with. He said that this particular genome would not respond well to the pharmaceutical approach. If I had undergone the treatment, I'd have exposed myself to debilitating side effects, some long-term, with little hope of success. Again the virus had offered me a gift—an increased confidence in my inner voice.

After I began using a breathing apparatus to help me with my sleep apnea, adopted transcendental meditation as a daily practice, and discovered that magnesium and vitamin E eliminated my restless leg syndrome, I was finally able get the rest I needed to continue with my recovery work. When I have difficulty sleeping now, it is because I haven't used all of the recovery tools at my disposal. I am continually humbled by life's reminders that becoming well is about progress, not perfection.

My desire to live with hepatitis C and be minimally affected by it has led to habits of caring for myself that are the exact opposite of the self-destructive tendencies of addiction. I can hardly believe I lived for so long in such despair and confusion. Structure and balance provide a blueprint for my days; they open up a world of choices by roping off the unhealthy ones at the get-go.

A typical day for me begins about 3:00 AM. That seems to be when my body wants to wake up, so I honour that. I've found that the darkness doesn't frighten me anymore, and the quiet stillness of the early morning is a perfect time for meditation, introspection, and creativity. When I swing my legs over the side of the bed, I do it with great energy, fuelled partly by gratitude. I remember well what it felt like to wake up in the morning wishing I'd died in my sleep. Digger greets me with sleepy eyes and a busy tail. While he's eating breakfast, I prepare a liver cleanse: the juice of an organic orange in two glasses of filtered water, and fifteen minutes later the juice of five good-sized carrots, half a head of celery, and several sprigs of parsley.

After meditating for twenty minutes, I set my intentions for the day, write them down, and release them to the universe. I say the Serenity Prayer, which asks my higher power to "grant me the serenity to accept the things I cannot change, the courage to change the things I can, and the wisdom to know the difference." I choose a daily reading from one of several books.

I pray for the strength not to medicate my feelings with food for that day only. The "one day at a time" slogan is one of the mainstays of my recovery. Trying to change the behaviour of a lifetime would be overwhelming, but dealing with just one day seems doable.

I write out my food plan for the day, noting everything that will go into my mouth. To treat my low blood sugar, I've found that eating three small meals and four snacks a day keeps my blood sugar stabilized and minimizes cravings. Recently I learned that saturated fat and salt stress the liver, so I've given up meat, salt, and dairy products. This was a difficult adjustment. I do allow myself the occasional treat of organic chicken, wild salmon, or cappuccino at my favourite café.

After a snack, usually organic peanut butter on homemade bread, I take a cup of tea upstairs to the computer. Digger follows and, as is our ritual, lays his substantial frame against my foot. He is my muse. When I first started to write, four years ago, I was driven, frantically pouring my life onto the page for fear I would lose my courage. Now I limit my writing to two or three hours a day, including editing from hard copy. My addict-self continually and vigorously resists a life of balance.

When I'm finished writing, I prepare all the food planned for the day, including snacks, wrap it, and put it in the fridge. This cuts down on impulse eating. Digger has been waiting patiently by the kitchen door, his tail swishing on the floor like a windshield wiper. When I reach for his leash he becomes a flurry of spins, leaps, rump gyrations, and yelps of delight. During our walk, I reflect on my day so far while he sniffs and anoints everything vertical, huffing and snorting at cats lolling on my neighbours' doorsteps along the way.

After breakfast, I go through my floor exercise routine and upper body workout, shower, tidy up, and head upstairs for another writing session. Once I've taken care of business matters, phone calls, and errands, I have lunch and walk Digger again. Having only recently given myself permission to rest in the afternoon ("the only thing worse than a drunk is a lazy one"), I set aside an hour or two for reading.

When the feelings surface—the sadness, the regret, the unresolved anger, the shame—I don't "get busy" to distract myself.

Suppressed feelings fester into insidious killing machines. I don't try to put them out of my mind. That can't be done. Thoughts and feelings come; there's no controlling them. I stop, sit down, feel the feelings, and write them down. It really works. Once I've done that not-so simple exercise I can go for a walk or play the piano—but not instead of feeling the feelings. If I nip things right away, I don't fall prey to the collecting tendencies of addiction. Addiction would have me believe that a big pile of resentments would be the perfect excuse for a relapse.

After meditation and supper, Digger and I go upstairs for our quiet time. He plops himself on the bed, hoping I'll forget that he usually sleeps downstairs on the couch. I read, watch the news, and have an early night. Just before I turn off the light, I go over my day—not to beat myself up for errors in judgment or a slip with my shopping or food abstinence, but only to be mindful of how I could do things differently tomorrow. If there are any amends I need to address or resentments that interfere with my serenity, I jot a note to myself to discuss them with a trusted recovery friend. Addiction likes to rationalize and deny, so second opinions are necessary. This daily routine rarely varies.

Each week I attend a group therapy session facilitated by Dr. Hajela. I've been going for almost nine years. It's a safe place, where addiction is continually exposed for what it is, in all its clever manifestations. We tell each other the truth, and when the pain of that is overwhelming we support each other, but never coddle.

Before I took my last drink I decided to avoid relationships with the opposite sex until I was well enough, and I have remained celibate for more than eight years now. Having never been engaged in a healthy relationship, and having never experienced consensual sex except when I was on some sort of medication, I decided to attend weekly twelve-step "relationship addiction" meetings. The discovery that I thoroughly enjoy my own company was quite a surprise.

A weekly routine for housework avoids the compulsive-cleaning trap, and I have learned to do some of my own main-

tenance work. Last summer I added a sledgehammer to my
growing collection of tools and laid a section of flagstone in
the garden, and I plan to ask Santa for a variable-speed drill
for Christmas. Until recently I was not physically able or
focused enough to consider such projects. I'm finally learning
to give my garden the attention and nourishment it needs, to
resist the inclination to yank and pull and force it to perform,
to just let it be. And so my life.

I had no idea how much time it would take to eat well. I
seek out organic produce at local farms and search vegetarian
cookbooks for tasty protein substitutes. To keep expenses
down, I buy seasonally to make huge pots of spaghetti sauce,
chili, baked beans, soups, and stew, for freezing in portion-
controlled servings. To avoid additives, preservatives, hidden
sugar, and pesticides that are harmful to my liver, I make my
own jam, ketchup, hot dog relish, chili sauce, salad dressings,
muffins, and bread—all from scratch. This keeps my diet as
liver-friendly as possible and holds sugar cravings at bay.

I see Dr. Hajela once a month for a private counselling session and visit the liver clinic every three months. Despite my
refusal to take the recommended pharmaceutical approach,
the doctors take good care of me, with regular liver enzyme
tests and ultra-sounds to screen for tumour activity. Liver can-
cer is more prevalent in hepatitis C patients.

Recovery is a full-time job, but a simple program. There are
things I can and cannot do. I am learning how to face life, how
not to medicate my feelings with food, alcohol, drugs, or nicotine. But substances aren't the only means of escaping life.
Behaviours such as shopping, all forms of busyness, playing
bingo, and buying lottery tickets are readily available traps for
me. Decades-old patterns of thinking—denial, criticism, judgment, manipulation, and avoidance—will resurface and lead
to a relapse if they're not attended to daily with recovery tools.

When I backslide with cigarettes or sugar, it is always
because I am trying to control how life happens instead of simply making sure that my *reaction* to what happens is healthy.
And honesty in all its forms is vital for me. I'm not aspiring to

sainthood—I know that my conscience has a low threshold for guilt and is easily offended. If I were to pile up too many offences, I would default to drinking or some other destructive behaviour. I know. It has happened to me countless times. There is no cure for this disease that uses substances and behaviours to suppress all feelings. It can only be managed with vigilance and perseverance.

So structure and discipline provide a circumference within which I can move freely. If a colt who sees the corral as restricting his freedom is released by his owner, he soon finds that he's hungry, he misses his friends, his hoofs become infected, he is attacked by wolves. He limps back home barely alive, and his owner opens the gate to the corral. Now he sees his home differently—not as restrictive, but as protective, comforting, safe. And he is now content to stay inside.

I have an honest, loving relationship with my family, and choose my friends with great care. By learning how to feel my feelings, I've come alive. I live a simple life, but a very exciting one. Thank God for relativity: after living in the dark for so long, even the tiniest candle seems to me a star. A simple task like using a caulking gun for the first time is a great adventure.

According to Dr. Hajela, I'm healthier now than I was when I was in my twenties, virus and all. Without hepatitis C, I would have been clean and sober, sort of happy, and almost free. Ho-hum happy is okay, and only a little enslavement is better than total bondage. But the gift pushed me into the freedom I'd only fantasized about, the joy I'd thought was only for other people.

§

Perhaps if I had not had the virus I would have gone back to using drugs and alcohol in order to face life. A return to drinking would lead to rapid decline and death. I'm on the cusp of liver failure. But I can stay that way for twenty years if I take care.

The virus holds me in a pattern of self-care and loving gestures toward myself. I've learned that there had been strength and discipline there all along, way down in a forgotten place. The gift of the virus gives me a reason to remember I was worth the effort and a reason to forget I ever thought I wasn't. My microscopic ally has helped me rise humbly in my own estimation, until sometimes I can barely remember how much I once loathed myself.

Where do I find the words to express how it feels to have a sun living inside of me? — an enchanted sun that softens my corners, smoothes my prickles, and adds a thousand new dimensions to my world. Freedom birthed my sun in the cosmos of my human heart, that vast vulnerable space where so much has been recorded. And it was only because I had been hobbled for half a century by a disease that robbed me of my self-respect that I could fully appreciate how it felt to be free.

My sun nudges me from the inside and helps me find great pleasure in the ordinary things I took for granted. Recently my friend David gave me a gift he had made himself, a colourfully painted ceramic pot filled with hand cream made of beeswax from his hives. I felt as though he'd handed me the world.

I feel like a child, eyes as big as saucers, discovering a life I had almost missed. My immense gratitude for a second chance transforms the mundane into an adventure. When despair has loomed for so long, a little joy seems colossal. When I emerged from the darkness of addiction, the first glint of light seemed a beacon that encouraged me onward. The light, of course, is the truth. It draws back the curtain and lets life in.

I'm saddened when I pass the man on a downtown street corner begging for money. He's the man who passed me my first bottle of sherry at the bootlegging establishment forty-five years ago. He sits in a wheelchair now, not physically disabled but crippled by the disease of addiction. He is glaringly absent from his body, missing from life, and he wears his slain heart on his face. He forgot who he was, and who he could be, just as I did. I'm deeply grateful for the quirks of chance that kept me from joining him on the street corner.

When my grandniece Holly calls me "Auntcey" and my brother calls me "Sweetie," they are not only words, but bits of affection that climb inside my ear and shape a sweet, soft, singing sound.

My clever sun shines acceptance on the past and reminds me how fortunate I am to be alive. It seeks out the most elusive of resentments and illuminates the shadows in the picture of my life. It defies cosmic law by shining day and night into a life that almost wasn't. The sun that sits in the core of me is pure, sweet joy.

It watches my dreams come true. One of these was to play the piano well enough that one day I could give a recital for my family. I'd taken lessons for a few years as a child, but I didn't like waiting in the chilly hall at the convent for the nun to call me in for a half-hour of torture. I didn't like her smacking my knuckles with a wooden ruler, and especially didn't like everyone making a federal case out of my hitting her back one day and knocking her off her chair.

Two decades later, in the desperate times, I found myself pretending that my family was sitting in the audience at Carnegie Hall, pride on their faces as they looked up at the stage. I played epic concertos, playful sonatas, and soulful rhapsodies with gusto, my arms whipping about as silent chords danced in the air. The vacancy in my spirit was filled by my brilliant performances before an admiring audience.

Three years into sobriety, I again found myself waiting for my teacher to begin a lesson. I tried to ignore my trembling knees. After interviewing several piano teachers, I had met Mark, a young, hip composer and a brilliant pianist, who appeared to be on a spiritual journey similar to mine. Our lessons were a little about the piano lesson but mostly about two people, each of whom found a kindred spirit in the other. Eventually we moved the lessons to my home, where we lingered over stimulating talks about music and life.

When I was growing up, Dad's easy chair sat in the corner directly behind me, and each time I made a mistake while practising I'd look around to see if he'd noticed. After his death, I still did. One day years later I was in the middle of the *Moonlight Sonata*, Dad's favourite piano piece, when an idea sent me racing down to the basement. I thrashed through boxes and bags ripe with mildew until I found what I was looking for. Waiting to come out of their exile were dozens of pictures of father and daughter, taken when they could still see each other over the walls they'd built. I chose several and dashed to the framing shop.

When they were ready, I placed them on the table exactly where Dad's chair used to be and said to his unsmiling, bearded face, "How could you have been the perfect father and human at the same time?"

Then I said to myself, standing beside him in the photograph, "How could you have been the perfect daughter and human at the same time?"

From then on, instead of looking around when I made mistakes, I smiled down at the keys and forgave myself. Only then could I turn to my father's picture and pardon his humanity, for I could not give to him what I had not already given to myself. Since then, I've spoken the same words a hundred times to those two people I was learning to accept and understand. Each time, another remnant of our past fell away.

My sun was there when another dream came true. My family was coming for Boxing Day and I was preparing a surprise for them, a piano recital that included Frank Mills's *Prelude in C*, *Ave Maria*, and *It's a Wonderful Life*.

Peter and Ann, my niece and nephew Susan and David, and their families piled in the door, stamping snow from their feet. Digger in his new Christmas scarf met them with a flurry of tail-wagging and rump gyrations. We nibbled on hors d'oeuvres as we opened our gifts, the air a-dance with genuine merriment. I was humbled to be able to rewrite our family's Christmas story—with me in it this time, sober and well.

It was time. I sat at the piano, as nervous as I'd ever been. I opened my music, positioned my hands on the keys, and began to play, my fingers wet with tears. It wasn't Carnegie Hall and I wasn't playing an epic concerto, but my audience was real, and so was the pride on their faces. As I realized my dream the past became irrelevant, and the spirit of Christmas embraced us all.

While the others were milling about, Peter mentioned that his favourite piano piece was *Liebestraum*. We found it in my *Easy Classical Selections* and I played the first few bars. "Yes, yes," he said. "That's it, you've got it." I promised him I would learn the piece, record it, and deliver the tape to him in a few weeks.

For a reason that escapes me, I mentioned to him that I'd had been envious of a steel moose he'd designed and given to our father years earlier. It felt good to share old things from a new perspective. Peter said, "I'll make you a moose." Maybe the unspoken words were, "I'm trying to shed the past too."

Peter had suffered from my addiction. We hadn't really quarrelled. When Dad died, I'd felt slighted by the conditions of his will and unconsciously blamed Peter. And just before Mom died, I'd been upset by a perfectly sound decision he'd made on her behalf. I was unable to discuss it with him when it happened, so time, sorrow, and self-loathing distorted the facts until there seemed to be a mountain of resentments between us. I thought he had abandoned me. I understand now that I had deserted myself, and in doing so I had alienated Peter. Both of us seemed unable to rid ourselves of each other's pain. The damage done to our relationship was not outright destruction, more like a gradual, devastating slide toward disconnection.

Peter nicknamed the gift to come "Moosey." Even his offering it to me lifted me up to a place only prodigal sisters would understand. By coming home to myself I had also opened the door for my brother. That day in the house where we both grew up, with the tree lights twinkling in celebration, we moved from dissonance to harmony and began to reclaim our sibling ties.

§

When my family left, I sat in my healing chair with Digger snuggled close. I thought about the house I was raised in and lived in now, having inherited it from my mother. This same house had listened to the story of our family all those years, and had kept its secrets well. It looked like any other on the outside, but it was now distinguished on the inside by hiding-closets, healing-chairs, and four-legged angels.

The house had been a watcher, a solemn witness, as I succumbed to a disease, an ailment of the brain and heart called addiction. It had watched itself being transformed into my own skid row, and watched me nearly give up on life. Then, miraculously, it had watched me healing within its walls. It watched me as I finally remembered who I was and began to write the story of my life in a steady, sober hand.

I thought about Christmas and how for me its essence wasn't found under the tree. The promises Peter and I made to each other that day were gap-closing gifts, the kind that act as a bridge between sibling ruins on distant shores. I thought about how families are watchers too, and how difficult it must have been for my family to watch someone they loved hurting herself repeatedly. My learning to play the piano, I realized, had little to do with the music and much to do with family mending.

Three months later I was on my way to Peter's home to deliver the tape of *Liebestraum*. The spring sun warmed the landscape. I pulled over by a fence where a chestnut mare stood heavy with new life. In the next field a group of men prepared the soil for planting. I felt tremendous gratitude for being able to see beyond the periphery of my own pain. And I couldn't wait to see Moosey.

As we lounged in the big room until dinner was ready, the effort to make me feel welcome was palpable. The air resounded with unspoken things—the desire to understand, to forgive, to rebuild. Later, shy, tentative exchanges wove through the laughter as carefully prepared dishes made their way around the table.

After dinner Peter said, "Let's go sit in my new truck. We can listen to your tape there." I knew our listening together was not all about the music. Neither of us said a word. It seemed that we were giving gifts to each other to show we still cared, until it felt safe to talk about the rift that had grown between us.

When the tape was over, Peter smiled and said, "Your play-ing is coming along nicely. I loved it. Thank you." We sat qui-etly for a moment. Then he said, "Let's go down to the base-ment."

There, on his workbench, was Moosey, all bright and shiny-smooth, standing two and a half feet tall and leaning at a uniquely creative angle. Dear silent Moosey, resonant with heart-words, now lives in front of my fireplace. And he is now a watcher too.

I began to study the original version of Liszt's *Liebestraum* for Peter's next birthday. It is a seven-page Grade 10 piece, and at that time I was playing at a Grade 4 level, so it would take a year to learn and memorize it. As I practised, I was aston-ished by the glorious living sound that rose from the keyboard.

When the piece was ready I rented recording equipment and prepared the tape of *Liebestraum* for Peter. But the real gift was a personal concert for him. We'd planned to meet at my house on his birthday. It was a fine June day, warm and still but for the wild beating of my heart. He sat behind me in an easy chair while I realized my dream. I gave him my gift, play-ing not in the air but on genuine ivory keys, and the audience this time was very real—my brother, lost and found.

§

My sun shines on the writing of this manuscript. Other than some dark poems I wrote in my teens, this is my first attempt at writing. The seed had been planted a few years before, but I had more healing work to do before I could tell my story from a recovering perspective. I began to write it after I met Marilyn, a feisty lawyer from California. We met in Alaska, when I was on a cruise. We started corresponding by e-mail, lengthy heart-felt outpourings about life and recovery. While rereading those e-mails, I noticed that I was able to express myself in a way that surprised me. It was time to tell the truth to myself.

My story is nearly told. But I've avoided the keyboard for a week, afraid I wouldn't be able to describe what joy felt like. Shame words and words describing pain came easily, and desperation words made my fingers fly. I had to record them first, or the final chapters would have had no meaning. I knew that the remembering and accepting of the past, without judgment or shame, was where my joy lived. I'd felt that joy swell and stretch, touching everything, adjusting the lens of my perception to an honest focus. I'd experienced, with wonder, how even things that appeared to be problematical made me feel alive in the solving of them. Yet the joy words stuck inside, afraid to come to the page for fear they would not be real.

When I first started writing my fingers trembled, astonished at what they were creating on the page, grateful to be finally getting the chance to lay the truth down so that I could pick up the next phase of my life. And the past fell between the lines and disappeared, down, down into a place where pasts are happy to go when the time is right.

But the fear still comes every morning, as I climb the narrow back stairs to the keyboard. I wonder if other writers fear that one day the reservoir of words will run dry.

It felt odd at first to refer to myself as a writer. On a conscious level I had not aspired to be a writer—in fact I hadn't even considered it. But as the years passed in recovery, my intuition continued to send me messages: I *must* write about my life, I must tell the story to myself, for my own healing. Although that was at first the sole purpose of my writing, as the manuscript evolved I began to experience a powerful sense that it would eventually help others.

The writing of this book has been a metaphor for my recovery process. When I reread the first three or four chapters of the first draft, I saw how short and timid the sentences were, much like my first steps into a world of reality. As I continued to write, I took more chances with words and poured out all the feeling I'd tried to suppress for five decades. Yet I still worried the words wouldn't come. I began setting an intention every morning before I placed my fingers on the keyboard that I would write from my heart with impeccable honesty, keeping my head out of it as best I could. And the joy words finally came to claim their rightful place in my manuscript.

I believe that in a sense this book is separate from me, its destiny having been decided long ago along with mine. We started out together, me living the life and the words telling the story. Now I must let it go, to be what it will be.

§

Sometimes my sun comes in extraordinary packages. One day while I was talking to my sister-in-law, Anne, she made an odd request. I was to measure the upstairs middle-front window of my home and report back to her. I was intrigued, and eagerly did what she asked.

The window measurements were six by four feet. At one time the two upper front rooms had been one large one with three windows. When the space was converted into two bedrooms, the middle window was bricked in. The frame and the limestone windowsill were left intact on the outside.

December 25th arrived and I drove to Peter and Ann's home. After a short visit, I was led to the basement. What I saw there lit me up brighter than any Christmas tree. Leaning against the wall was a portrait of Digger and me. Ann had painted me sitting down, wearing my favourite outfit, a camel pant and vest outfit, with an ivory blouse, long since worn out, and Digger was looking up adoringly. Ann had captured perfectly how I gaze at him with wonderment and gratitude. She'd painted a faint golden glow around Digger's body, a perfectly captured radiance. Her plan was that this picture would make it appear that Digger and I were sitting in the window.

I waited till spring for the installation. Unable to find a window to protect the portrait and match the other two at the front, I decided to remove one from the back of the house and use it.

Digger always became nervous and watchful when he sensed I was upset with someone, and when the man installing the window dropped it, smashing the glass, Digger picked up on my anxiety. When the man got down on all fours to pick up the pieces of glass, Digger used his very solid snout to butt him on his backside. The man fell forward, sprawling like

Bambi. He wasn't hurt, and Digger's tail was wagging all the while, but it was a tense moment nonetheless.

My sun was shining again when the picture travelled up the ladder on a makeshift pulley. I had hung a fringed blind that matched the other windows, and Ann's plan was a smashing success. The sun was there when people stopped to point at this painting of a dog and a woman in the window. In the past, before the dog came, they would have been stopping and staring at an ambulance parked in front of the house, or a fire truck pumping water to an upstairs bedroom, or a woman who had fallen asleep on her front doorstep on a winter's day wearing only her nightgown and a pair of rubber boots. Now they stop to admire a picture of a dog and a woman who found hope when they found each other.

Digger's reaction to the people who stop to look at the picture is comical. Being the best watchdog in town, he bolts to the window just below the portrait. When he puts his paws on the sill most of his substantial body can be seen from the street. Tail wagging furiously, he barks and huffs and snuffs. The onlookers' heads go from the portrait to Digger, back up to the portrait, then back down again to Digger. When they realize he is the dog in the painting, they laugh and point again, which makes Digger even more indignant. Sometimes, just for fun, I stand in the window too.

§

My sun was there bright and summer-warm the day I joined Peter and Ann at my parents' Devil Lake property. Mom and Dad had been dead for several years, but their memories hung in the sticky, heavy air as we sorted and cleaned. We looked through old photographs, faded and dusty-yellow, peeling away from the pages. I sensed that it was the perfect time for me to see those pictures.

There was a picture of Dad cradling me when I was a baby. He seemed to gaze down at me, as if he were holding God's grace in his arms. It was 1945, just after the war, and hopes for his family were evident on his handsome face. His bow tie sat pertly on his collar, and his moustache was trimmed just right. Years later he would let me scratch those stiff hairs and he would throw his head back and laugh, a deep-rich father-mountain sound, pretending I was the best tickler a little girl could be. He loved me then. Neither the innocent child nor the fine, optimistic man could possibly have known that a disease called addiction would devastate their lives.

I was able to remember him that day, in the depth and breadth and length of his humanity. And love him more truly than ever before.

§

My sun was exceptionally talented. Its radiance germinated seeds of thought that sprouted roots to connect me to my higher power, to the earth, and to all living things. My lost sense of self had set me apart from things good and true for my whole life. Now it began to develop threads that pulled the errant, fragmented pieces into my centre and wove them carefully, lovingly into one sane human shape.

I had started having a recurring dream in my twenties, when my world was part fantasy and part hell. It developed into a frequent waking mind-excursion that made me smile and feel useful for a time.

I'm certain it was events in the early sixties that triggered this dream, which evolved into a forty-year fantasy. My father had responded to the Bay of Pigs crisis by stocking supplies in the basement in case of a nuclear attack, cases of beans and corn, matches, lanterns and pails, shovels and rope. In my dream a bomb had been dropped, and although I had been spared, the rest of my family were injured. I carried everyone to the basement, and just as they were resting comfortably, part of the ceiling collapsed and sealed off the opening to the outside world. We needed medical supplies, so I dug a trench leading out of the basement and connected it to the hospital, four blocks away. I crawled back and forth to the hospital foraging for medicine and bandages, prepared food from the supplies Dad had stored, and cared for my family until they were well.

As I remembered how it felt in the dream to be helpful instead of a burden, the dream would slip into a waking respite from the awful truth of my life. Several times a week, until my birthday this year, I would escape to that a make-believe time when I was a comfort to my family. My sun was there this year when I stood at the mailbox reading a card that Peter and Ann sent for my birthday. The last line of the message said, "We wish to let you know that you are a blessing too." The word "blessing" had been under-lined, and tiny red hearts were drawn around it. Knowing that my brother and sister-in-law didn't say or do anything they did not mean, I was deeply moved by that gesture. My heart, get-ting rather used to tumbling in and out of my chest in response to the joy in my life, leaped clear in the air and performed a perfect somersault.

A few days later Peter and Ann drove from their home a hundred miles away to wish me happy birthday. In times past I'd not always been a person one would wish to be around, and it was not as if they had time to make the trip on a work-day. So when they walked into my home, it seemed as though they'd tied love up in a bow and hung it on my door.

Then I received a birthday call from my nephew, who had-n't pretended for a moment that he didn't hate my disease. I didn't think he liked me much; I loved him deeply. We'd barely spoken for years, which had caused a chronic ache in my chest. When I heard his voice I thought I'd levitate. The grati-tude I felt as we said goodbye was vital to sustaining my sun's brilliance. I was again humbled by the process of recovery.

As I sat in my healing chair at the end of that day, I reviewed the last few years. I felt rounded, finished, filled in, as if the dots of our family had been joined. The promises of recovery were fulfilled only after I had done the necessary work.

In years gone by, being a blessing to my family had only been a fantasy, an escape from a life gone amiss. Having faced life, I am now allowed to take my place in the family album, and to be a person who brings joy to the familial table. I don't have to fantasize anymore. I am part of my tribe at last.

Afterword

These chapters illustrate that no life can sink so deeply into despair, and no spirit can ever become so mangled, that it cannot be mended by a humble act of surrender and a heartfelt wish to be whole.

My quest is simply to be real. For me, that means facing life head on, accepting the past, searching through the mist of denial for the truth. The truth I find will occasionally challenge my sanity and sobriety, but now I have the tools with which to respond to it. I am no longer willing to live on the surface of life. I must get under the skin of it, hunt down each resentment, search out each snippet of my past, for that is where the insufferable sound lived. And joy needs the truth to survive.

I hope this book will help others who are addicted. I humbly offer the example of my life to show that happiness can be had with a few changes in perspective and behaviour. The experience, strength, and hope of others in recovery is always there to guide me. All I need to do is ask. Help is available for everyone, and it costs nothing except the desire to be well. This help is loving, intelligent, and heartfelt. I offer the truth of my life to show how easily addiction can be triggered, and how it can entangle a life, then strangle it, without missing a step on its unconscionable way.

I am not special. I am a recovering addict who nearly died from lack of knowing how not to, and then came alive in the process of recovery. My journey through the maze of addiction may appear to be an ugly thing. I guess it just depends on who is looking. Mine is a story of sadness and fear, hope and joy — everyone's story. The feelings are the same for us all, only the details are different.

Recovery is a structured environment, a safe enclosure within which I can be totally free. It is a simple program. There are things I must do if I am to stay well, and things I must not do. Apart from those boundaries, a world of choices awaits me.

When I sit in my healing chair, I wonder about many things, including the end of my life. I'd be content to be remembered as honest and kind. That's all. The wild, unrealistic dreams I had as a young person about romantic love, success in the eyes of others, and material things have been replaced by the intention to live one day at a time with honour. Not big honour, but the kind that covers me kindly as I fall asleep at night, knowing that I did my best to live with integrity that day.

When I contemplate my life — how I tried to buck it, how it adhered tenaciously, how I will never again treat it carelessly — there is one thing I don't wonder about at all, and that is what will become of me. I may die in my sleep tonight, but if I don't, I know exactly what tomorrow will bring. As long as I stay on my recovery path and continue to face life, my tomorrows will be just like my todays, abounding with self-respect, peace, and joy.

Postscript

Addiction and Recovery: Clinical Perspectives
Raju Hajela

Life is a process. It is what happens to us. More importantly, though, it is what we do with what happens to us, with us, and by us. Nancy's story is about her process, her journey into finding her authentic self despite the challenges that came her way through various life events.

I met Nancy in 1997, at a time when she was struggling, yet trying really hard to present an image to the world that she was doing all right. She had been looking at many spiritual matters and was earnestly trying to apply the principles in her life. She was also full of fear and shame. She knew she wanted some help, yet there was also that desire to do it "myself ... in my own way." There was the longing to get rid of the pain that she was carrying. That pain was physical, mental, emotional, social, and spiritual. It was related to various life events, but it was largely emanating from a disease called addiction.

Every day, addiction-related events make news: accidents related to the use of alcohol and/or drugs, trafficking in illicit drugs, many other legal and legislative issues, and chronic strife in its various forms, including interpersonal violence. Addiction presents its face every day in the office of every doctor, psychologist, social worker, and lawyer. Yet it remains unaddressed, while the well-meaning professionals try to provide means of coping with the complications in the face of devastation. Only a fraction of the people who need help get it, largely because of confusion surrounding what addiction is and what resources are required for definitive interventions.

Addiction is a disease that appears wilful but in reality has an automaticity, which reflects a "loss of control." The person suffering from it and those around, including helping professionals, often try to educate the person into behaving better. Yet the disease can be dealt with only when people come to accept its nature, stop trying to control it, surrender to the process, and embrace recovery.

In 1999, the Canadian Society of Addiction Medicine defined addiction as follows:

> A primary, chronic disease characterized by impaired control over the use of a substance and/or behaviour. Clinically, the manifestations occur along biological, psychological, sociological, and spiritual dimensions. Common features are change in mood, relief from negative emotions, provision of pleasure, pre-occupation with the use of substance(s) or ritualistic behaviour(s); and continued use of the substance(s) and/or engagement in behaviour(s) despite adverse physical, psychological, and/or social consequences. Like other chronic diseases, it can be progressive, relapsing, and fatal.

Biologically, the disease has a genetic predisposition that becomes manifest through a sensitivity and a self-consciousness that can often alternate between feeling very vulnerable and inadequate, and feeling all-powerful to control and manipulate situations. The use of substances and the engagement in behaviours that are addictive further reinforce patterns in the brain circuitry such that the person appears more and more driven. The 1990s were an exciting decade with respect to research that has clarified the neurochemical pathways that are involved in the establishment and perpetuation of the disease of addiction. These pathways involve the hypothalamus, the part of the brain that is central to regulation of "appetites" or desire. Further, they are intricately connected to the feeling centres in the brain in the frontal and temporal regions of the cortex. Current evidence indicates that the changes at the level of neuronal pathways are irreversible. Thus, people with a high degree of genetic predisposition have altered pathways to begin with, and repeated engagement in addictive behaviour and the use of psychoactive substances sensitize and reinforce the brain circuitry that creates the automaticity of the disease of addiction. Physical illnesses often follow acutely or chronically, as complications from the use of substances and/or trauma resulting from engagement in high-risk behaviours. Infectious diseases and organ damage, especially to the liver, are common sequelae.

Psychologically, the cognitive (thinking) and affective (feeling) processes become more and more affected as the disease progresses. The sensitivity and vulnerability, which are hard to acknowledge, continue to worsen as the person is unable and/or unwilling to seek appropriate support to deal with the problems. The accumulation of emotional wreckage personally and the deep awareness of causing harm to others, in the absence of proper help, only increases the utilization of defence mechanisms of rationalization, projection, minimization, and denial. A process of increasing distortion of reality that is characterized by self-deception and lying to others begins, and is reinforced. It is sometimes said that the letters in the word "DENIAL" stand for "Don't Even kNow I Am Lying." There is increasing isolation from the outside world even when the person may appear to be surrounded by friends and family. There is a growing disconnection from the realities of life, such that the "fantasy" world of distorted thoughts and feelings becomes the internal reality from which and in reaction to which the addict responds and mostly reacts.

Socially, the person feels increasingly uncomfortable with the real world. Hence, the social circles that are sought and maintained are the ones that enable the disease to progress. These social circles are commonly of other addicts, and they also include family members and friends who try to smooth over problems because of their own fears, guilt, and shame. The psychological isolation also reinforces the social isolation. The behaviour resulting from the psycho-social aspects of addiction usually alienates the healthier social circles and perpetuates the disease process. This often results in the addict's listening to other people who are sick more than to a person who may be making a healthy suggestion. Even when a person gets into recovery, he or she will often gravitate toward someone else in early recovery who still carries significant distortion, and feel alienated from those further along in recovery. It is truly a remarkable phenomenon that in recovery people become closest to the people whom they had initially disliked!

Spiritually, the person loses connections with the inner self and the sense of belonging in this universe. There is a loss of values such that the person takes risks and engages in behaviour that may be morally reprehensible under usual circumstances. This contributes to increasing problems with shame and loss of self-esteem.

Nancy's story illustrates the various aspects of addiction. It is an honest account of how she interpreted and tried to cope with her life circumstances. She had loving parents, yet she suffered emotional trauma. No one was able to protect her from sexual trauma. She looked for comfort in dealing with the pain that results from the trauma, unmet needs and feelings that are hard to face. As a little girl, as Nancy describes, she did not have the means, nor the support, to deal with the fear and shame that resulted from her getting caught up in doing some things that were "bad." She found ways of escape.

People begin to look for escape as a coping mechanism, a way to survive. However, in time the escape becomes an entity of its own. When a person begins to use an escape as a comfort or a means of coping, he or she does not have much inkling of the entity that the escape will become. Insidiously, the escape repeated over time takes hold in the form of addiction. Over time, the harmful consequences to the individual, and to his or her family, friends, community, and workplace, accumulate repetitively and sequentially. All the while, the hiding, the self-deception, and the dishonesty with others prevent the individual from facing the realities of his or her life. The pain that one was trying to cope with and/or escape from becomes greater. Strangely enough, the more determined and intelligent a person is, the longer it takes for the harmful consequences to become significant enough to break the barrier of self-deception or denial. Wilfulness and determination feed denial, such that persons suffering from addiction, the addicts, are better able to hide from others and themselves.

Other people often offer sympathy and what they perceive as support in the form of attempts to keep things calm in the midst of mounting chaos. However, offering sympathy, rescuing the individual, and/or protecting the individual from facing the consequences of the disease only creates more denial. It sets up an insidious cycle of control and counter-control within and around the person suffering from addiction. The intense preoccupation with someone else's thoughts, feelings, and/or behaviour in an effort to change the individual "for the better" is commonly known as co-dependence. Unrealistic expectations and reactivity on the part of the addict and co-dependents around him or her create a negative spiral. The persons trying harder to be "good" repeatedly come up against the "loss of control," and "fail" to meet the expectations set up by themselves and others around them. This further increases shame and anger that is both self-directed and directed at others. The others involved in the cover-up also get frustrated from time to time and explode. This often induces remorse for over-reacting, and further protecting and rescuing follows. Thus, people caught up in this dance accomplish exactly the opposite of what they intend. They want the person to change; the person tries hard to change; yet the dynamics of control and counter-control only feed the disease of addiction and co-dependence. The definitive solution lies in surrender. This does not mean taking no action to counter the disease. Rather, it means taking action to learn about the nature of the disease. It involves exploration of the biological, psychological, social, and spiritual aspects of the disease that give it power and automaticity. It means developing a relationship with oneself, others, and the rest of the universe in the context of a power greater than oneself. It requires recognition that using willpower to control addiction is like holding the anal sphincter really tightly to control diarrhea!

Learning about the nature of the disease and taking appropriate action to deal with the issues requires commitment, honesty, and effort that initially appear monumental. Through practice, and learning from the obstacles encountered over time, people come to appreciate what is within their domain to change and what needs to be left alone as other people's issues and/or as in the hands of the God of one's understanding. This powerful concept is the cornerstone of the Twelve-Step program, which was started as Alcoholics Anonymous in 1935 by Bill W. and Dr. Bob S. Since then the program has found applicability in all other aspects of addiction beyond alcohol. These aspects include the use of other mood-altering substances—opioids, marijuana, other hallucinogens, tranquilizers (benzodiazepines and barbiturates), stimulants (cocaine, nicotine, amphetamines, etc.), and volatile organic compounds such as glue and gasoline—that people start to take to "escape" or change their mood. Further, people have come to realize that food, sex, the Internet, computer/video games, gambling (especially bingo and lotteries), relationships, exercise, and work can also become problematic as addiction for people who start to use them as "escape." The twelve steps provide a framework for the recognition of the problems one is "powerless" over and the unmanageability created by attempts to control; for connecting with a higher power; and for beginning the healing journey through personal responsibility for solutions that are within one's domain of action.

Nancy describes how the Twelve-Step program began to provide some structure and meaning to her life, which translated into recovery and a better quality of life. The first step, with its emphasis on acknowledgement of powerlessness over addiction and coming to appreciate the unmanageability of one's life, highlights the need for help from others and/or a higher power. There is recognition of the need for honesty, open-mindedness, and willingness. Rather than fearing others and expecting judgment, one starts to open up to the possibility that others may offer something that can be of benefit. It is difficult, because emotionally traumatized people are more familiar with being hurt by those who offered love and support. It is really challenging for those suffering from addiction to face the realities of their disease and become willing to trust others. Over time, people come to appreciate a sense of a higher power working in their lives through other people! This is a spiritual transformation in its earliest stages. As much as a lot of people equate spirituality with religion, it must be recognized that following a religious doctrine is not a necessary part of this spiritual appreciation. The spiritual is the recognition of connectedness, of something greater than the immediately obvious sum of various parts. In many instances a focus on religion rather than spirituality can be a hindrance. Most people suffering from addiction have a great sense of shame connected with the religion that they were exposed to during their formative years. People are sometimes traumatized by the control aspects of many religious practices, and/or carry a great sense of shame from not having lived up to the prescribed religious tenets. In either case, a general re-evaluation and a simpler approach from the perspective of basic spirituality remains critical. In time, people sometimes go back to their former religious doctrine, or adopt one closer to their renewed sense of self and values. At its foundation, this is spiritual regeneration, which is further consolidated for people in steps two and three of a Twelve-Step program.

The action steps, four through nine, provide a framework for the addict in recovery to face his or her emotional pain. Often, individual and group psychotherapy is required for an extended period of time. The intensity can vary from daily to weekly, but the need remains indefinitely because of the chronic nature of this disease. The treatment setting can also vary from just the community (the social-spiritual support of a Twelve-Step network), to outpatient treatment (of variable intensity), to residential treatment, to in-patient hospitalization, to extended periods of time in a therapeutic community. Invariably, treatment and recovery need to be tailored to the individual: each person cannot be expected to fit into the same prescribed treatment box. Nancy's recovery journey well illustrates the complementarities of various different things that appealed to her that she has been able to weave into a recovery program for herself.

The maintenance process is established through steps ten, eleven, and twelve. It takes a minimum of two years, and usually five years, for people to be truly in the maintenance stage of their recovery. Most often people keep encountering deeper and deeper layers of their addiction-related issues. It requires great vigilance and constant practice for people to remember their boundaries, to avoid falling prey to people-pleasing, and to acknowledge errors without heaping guilt and shame on themselves.

Recovery is a personal journey and it is multi-modal. Some people may not use the twelve steps as part of their process; however, the principles of the twelve steps are a universal template for recovery. Further, the Twelve-Step network offers a readily available nurturing and a relatively healthier social milieu, which is necessary to counteract the chaos in the social circles of an active addict. Among my patients there are several who have not followed the structure of the Twelve-Step program. Invariably, though, all that are stable in recovery continue to follow the same principles, which are rooted in self-awareness, honesty, acceptance, and humility.

Addicts display a lot of "all or nothing" thinking, which pervades every aspect of their lives. Relationships are as volatile as they are intense. There are often no boundaries, such that everyone is caught up in everyone else's issues, and/or there is a lot of pretense, and a neglect of real responsibilities. It is quite challenging for people in recovery to clarify what individual responsibility is all about. It takes time to learn that the "blame game" of projecting fault onto others or heaping it all on oneself is part of the dysfunction related to addiction and co-dependence. It takes a lot of practice to appreciate that one needs to stay within one's own boundaries as a sign of respect, even though it feels like "not caring" about others, in contrast to the fuzzy boundaries, where everyone gets into everyone's business while neglecting his or her own responsibilities. It requires a quantum shift to appreciate that boundaries are not rejection. Assertiveness about expressing one's feelings and clarifying healthy boundaries actually promotes honesty and trust, and ultimately fosters genuine connectedness, trust, and sense of community.

Nancy's story illustrates all of the above aspects of addiction and the challenges of being human in the quest of individuation of oneself and maintenance of the connection with the rest of the universe. Her journey is mapped out in graphic detail. It has served to bring clarity to her. In her sharing this with others, she has been able to let go of what others may or may not think of her. It has led to the diminishing of shame and the healing of the emotional pain of isolation.

I am glad to be a part of Nancy's recovery journey. I hope her recounting of her journey in these pages will serve as an inspiration to those who are themselves suffering from addiction and/or know someone who is. Addiction is such a common disease that none of us has to look far among our family and friends to find someone affected; and it is humbling to appreciate that all of us are affected quite directly. May the understanding and joy reflected in Nancy's story provide hope as a counterpoint to suffering.

DR. RAJU HAJELA received his MD from Dalhousie University in 1982 and his MPH from the Harvard School of Public Health in 1988. His undergraduate studies were in physics, and he has maintained an interest in that subject, especially as its concepts are related to consciousness and health. He has practised Transcendental Meditation since 1986, and he completed training in Maharishi Ayurveda in 1994. He is a Certificant and Fellow of the College of Family Physicians of Canada and of the American Society of Addiction Medicine, and a Certificant of the Canadian Society of Addiction Medicine and of the International Society of Addiction Medicine. He has held academic appointments and leadership positions in national and international medical organizations, specializing in addiction medicine and physician health. He practised in Kingston, Ontario, from 1991 to 2006. His current consulting practice includes occupational health, and individual and group psychotherapy, with integrated Ayurvedic concepts, for the treatment of addiction and chronic non-cancer pain, in Calgary, Alberta.

FACING LIFE
Nancy Brown
First edition · First printing

Facing Life was designed and typeset by Dennis Choquette at Penumbra Press, in Manotick, Ontario. The type is Linotype Sabon (11/13.5), which was designed by Jan Tschichold and first issued in 1964. The paper is Rolland Enviro 100, an acid-free, ancient-forest-friendly paper milled in Saint-Jérôme, Québec.

The cover features a detail of a painting by Wilfrid Flood titled *Henrietta Tremblay* (1928 · watercolour on paper · 22″ × 16½″).

Copy-editing: Douglas Campbell
Proofreading: Dennis Choquette
Printing: Tri-Graphic, Ottawa